Writer's Guide

THE ESSENTIAL POINTS

Harold H. Kolb Jr.

University of Virginia

HARCOURT BRACE JOVANOVICH, INC.

New York San Diego Chicago San Francisco Atlanta
London Sydney Toronto

This work is dedicated to students in Charlottesville and judges in Nashville, without whom it would not have been possible, or necessary.

ISBN: 0-15-597680-X

Library of Congress Catalog Card Number: 80-80390

Printed in the United States of America

Preface

I began this book as a guide for undergraduate majors in American Studies at the University of Virginia. Although they had breezed through, struggled through, slept through, or been exempted from the freshman composition course, many still needed assistance with their writing, especially as their assignments became more demanding. Then I was asked to conduct several seminars in opinion writing for the American Academy of Judicial Education, and I discovered that judges and lawyers had many problems in common with serious college students. There is, I have come to learn, an army of intelligent Americans, in schools and in professions, who need help in improving their writing. With this audience in mind, I have attempted to present a reasonable discussion of the rules for good writing—one that takes a stand that is balanced, moderate, practical; and one that gives some notion of the reasons for the rules.

I am grateful for advice, however perversely I may have employed it, from L. A. Beaurline, Richard Bullock, Drake Bush, Hoyt Duggan, Robert Hoyt, William J. Kerrigan, Sandra Lifland, Tom Miles, Philip Ressner, Dana Roeser, and—first and last—Jean Burgin Kolb. Judge Leonard Martin, of Charlotte, Tennessee, kindly allowed me to print the excerpt on page 15. The manuscript was expertly typed by Karen Carter and Trixie de Winter.

H. H. K.

Contents

Preface   iii
Introduction   vii

Absolute expressions	1
Adjectives and adverbs	1
Ambiguity	1
Capitalization	3
Clichés	4
Coherence	7
Conciseness	10
Connection	13
Dictionaries	17
Etymology	19
Exceptions	24
False comparative	26
Footnote and bibliographic forms	26
Form and content	31
Grammar, usage, and style	32
Handbooks	37
Homonyms	39
Jargon	40
Latinisms	43
Literary writing and expository writing	45
Metaphor	47
Neologism	50
Numbers	51
Obvious statements	51
Paragraphing	52

Parallelism   56
Precision   58
Pronouns   59
Proofreading   61
Puffery   62
Punctuation   62
Quotations   68
Revision   70
Sexist language   71
Slang   72
Specific details   74
Speech and writing   76
Spelling   76
Thesis   78
Titles   80
Typing conventions   80
Usage: some particular cases   81
Variety   92
Verbs   94
Weak intensifiers   95

Afterword   97
Index   99

Introduction

Books about writing often make dismal reading, partly because they attempt to cover all rules for all writers. In spite of sections labeled "conciseness" or "bloated language," writing texts themselves are packed with too much terminology, too many examples, too many refinements that a writer seldom needs. They veer from catchy analogies—a good sentence is like a good golf swing—to grandiose declamations: "The writing of English is a moral matter." In spite of injunctions concerning "tone," writing manuals are often rigidly prescriptive, condescending, and negative. Like William Holmes McGuffey's *Eclectic Readers,* they bristle with "Faults to be Remedied," beating the joy out of language and reducing it to a dull series of rules. Some rules are needed—no one plays tennis with the net down—but if they are tiresome the text is at fault, not the language. Seventy-five per cent of the useful suggestions for good writing can be summarized in about one hundred pages; the other twenty-five per cent take five hundred. This guide attempts to state briefly the main points and is addressed to the intermediate writer—the person who has a subject and can recognize a sentence, whose goal is to make his or her writing more accessible, more effective, more persuasive. These suggestions are meant to help the student understand principles of composition and customs of usage without feeling bound by inflexible rules, to help him balance the opposed virtues of convention and innovation, constraint and freedom, regulation and release.

Good writing begins with something to say, and ends in communication. It conveys the author's meaning by creating signals that allow the reader to move from point to point with ease and understanding. There are many ways to create these signals effectively, but most employ the following elements:

1. *Coherence* Grouping parts of sentences, paragraphs, and essays appropriately, consistently, logically

2. *Connection* Creating bridges between parts by employing linking words and repetitions

3. *Precision* Using exact words and expressions

4. *Conciseness* Eliminating the unnecessary

5. *Correctness* Choosing appropriate grammar and usage

Other elements of good writing can be identified that lean toward persuading a reader, keeping his attention:

6. *Variety* Creating interestingly diverse phrases and sentences

7. *Specificity* Anchoring the balloon of generalization with concrete, particularized detail

The line between communication and persuasion is often blurred. Yet an author can usually assume that if his writing is persuasive, the reader is likely to be receptive to its meaning; if his writing conveys its meaning efficiently, that very quality will help to persuade.

Each of these seven elements is discussed in the text under the entries listed in parentheses: *coherence* (Ambiguity, Coherence, Paragraphing, Parallelism, Thesis); *connection* (Connection); *precision* (Clichés, Homonyms, Jargon, Neologism, Precision, Puffery, Slang); *conciseness* (Adjectives and adverbs, Conciseness, Latinisms, Obvious statements, Weak intensifiers); *correctness* (Capitalization; False comparative; Footnote and bibliographic forms; Grammar, usage, and style; Numbers; Pronouns; Proofreading; Punctuation; Quotations; Spelling; Titles; Typing conventions; Usage: some particular cases); *variety* (Variety); and *specificity* (Specific details).

Advice to writers, like other kinds of advice, should be honest, dealing with the world inhabited by the writer, not with an academic Shangri-La. It ought to be flexible, making recommendations without slamming the door on choice. It ought to be informative, letting the reader see through to the principles behind good writing and the history behind conventions of usage. And it can be enjoyable. Even Koko, the seven-year-old subject of a Stanford University experiment in teaching sign language to anthropoid apes, seems to have discovered the fun of irony, argument, humor, rhyme, and swearing. This guide takes for one of its premises the notion that the pleasures of language exist for literate humans as well as literate gorillas.

Absolute expressions—*all, always, every, invariably, never, none, totally, undoubtedly*—should be used with a light hand. They are, in the first place, rarely accurate, for most human truths are of the seventy-five per cent variety. And absolutes tend to trigger the reader's perversity; once told that "the campaign was a total failure," he or she begins to hunt for signs of partial success, for loopholes in the wall of totality. If you use such expressions, be prepared to defend them.

But don't slide to the other extreme and turn your writing to mush with soft qualifications: *almost, fairly, for the most part, nearly, occasionally, often, partially, perhaps, possibly, probably, sometimes, usually.* State your points firmly, directly, crisply. Use qualifications and absolutes when they are needed, but don't make either device a characteristic feature of your writing—or your thinking.

Adjectives and adverbs are minor characters in the drama of the English language. They can add a colorful touch, a clearer focus, a sharpened edge, but they should not be allowed to upstage the main actors—nouns and verbs. "His actual knowledge of the case is extremely limited as far as the real facts are concerned" should be boiled down to its essence: "He has limited knowledge of the facts of the case." Avoid especially the stop-and-go sentence whose every part is constantly qualified with cumbersome baggage.

A writer turns to adjectives and adverbs in an attempt to strengthen a statement. "He is a fast decision maker" becomes "He is clearly a very fast decision maker." A revision that energizes the verb provides strength without clutter: "He makes decisions rapidly."

See **Conciseness, Verbs, Weak intensifiers.**

Ambiguity as a term in literary criticism refers to richness and complexity, to Melvillean layers beneath layers, but by that

the critic means intentional, controlled ambiguity. Uninten-
tional ambiguity is the writer's curse. "Napoleon declared
himself emperor in pursuit of his goals." The general meaning
is more or less clear, but there is a momentary uncertainty
whether "Napoleon" or "emperor" is doing the pursuing,
whether Napoleon declared himself "emperor" or "emperor in
pursuit of his goals." The sentence leaps in two directions at
once and the reader is in danger of either getting stuck at the
crossroads or following the wrong path. "Gov. Lamar
Alexander canceled his engagement to tour the flood-stricken
area." This dispatch leaves us guessing whether the governor
canceled an office appointment or his tour.

The *Tennessee Code Annotated* specifies a twelve-month
period in which owners may sue for damage to their property,
with the exception of "unknown owners and nonresidents,"
who have a longer period. Ever since the law was written,
judges have wrestled with the meaning of the exception:

> There is some confusion as to the terminology in the statute
> when it refers to "unknown owners and nonresidents." Did the
> drafters of the law intend to make unknown owners and
> nonresidents conjunctive? *(Chumney vs. South Central Bell,*
> Tenn. Ct. of App. W.S., 1977)

A simple "or" instead of "and" would have signified the
drafters' apparent intent that a person claiming the exception
must be either an unknown owner or a nonresident, but need
not be both; it would have saved many pages of judicial
commentary and many hours of judicial time.

Much of the confusion in prose results from the loss of
signals when speech is translated into writing. "The plaintiff
contends the hospital may be partially responsible for the
damages and should be in this case." A speaker would say

"and *should* be in this case," if he means that the hospital should be considered partially responsible in this instance. He would say "and should be *in* this case" if the meaning is that the hospital should be a party to the suit. "In teaching business writing instructors often use case studies." A speaker of that sentence would invariably pause between "writing" and "instructors." Stripped of the eloquence of vocal emphasis and tone, the subtle telegraphy of eye contact, and the meaning conveyed in what is interestingly and accurately called body English, writing has to be more explanatory, coherent, connected, and precise than speech.

A reader, sandbagged by ambiguity, is likely to complain that the writer "doesn't know what he is talking about." Usually the reverse is true. The writer knows exactly what he is talking about and therefore finds no confusion in sentences that the reader, with less knowledge, must puzzle over. The writer must try to see his prose as others see it; he must work constantly to lead the reader down a single, straight, seemingly inevitable track. While the strait and narrow is no easier in prose than in conduct, writing at least can be revised. In the heat of composition the writer need not be bothered by the possibility of ambiguity, of multiple paths. In the cool tranquility of revision he goes back to block the wrong exits.

See **Coherence, Pronouns, Revision, Speech and writing.**

Capitalization.   The essence of capitalization is specificity. If you are referring to a single, specific, unique entity *(the West, President Carter, Mother Grundy, the Mississippi Valley)* use a capital letter. It is not necessary for a general reference *(traveling west, one of several presidents, my friend's mother, a peaceful valley).* Specific centuries *(sixteenth-century drama, the eighteenth century)* are exceptions to this principle, perhaps because a large specific tends to overflow into generality.

Usage is divided on two issues—capitalized nouns converted to adjectives, and designations of race. In the first issue most publishers seem to use the upper case: *Southern cooking*. In the second, consistency provides a guide: *Caucasian, Negro; white, black*.

Clichés are expressions that have lost their freshness through repetition, as the word's etymology suggests (from the French *clicher,* to cast a printing plate—called a stereotype). Many had brilliant beginnings as original metaphors and similes. The Paleolithic hunter who first reported that his gnawed bone was clean as a whistle really had something, but his phrase has been worn thin by countless millions of repetitions.

Everyone is familiar with these expressions; familiarity is precisely the problem:

add insult to injury	last but not least	spur of the moment
bitter end	nick of time	
blind as a bat	once and for all	straw that broke the camel's back
crack of dawn	pitch black	trying times
crystal clear	sharp as a tack	turn for the worse
dawn of history	slow but sure	white as snow
fate worse than death	smooth as glass	
first and foremost	soft as silk	

Another list of expressions could be compiled that, though

they fall short of the lacquered finality of clichés, are repeated too often for comfort:

absolute minimum

all intents and purposes

at great length

at this point in time

benefit of the doubt

bewildering variety

circumstances beyond his control

contagious enthusiasm

devil's advocate

dire consequences

drastic mistake

dubious distinction

early on

for all practical purposes

for the foreseeable future

generally regarded

healthy skepticism

idle speculation

innocent bystander

inordinate amount

intestinal fortitude

in the final analysis

invidious distinction

keenly attuned

lifestyle

mutual advantage

no uncertain terms

outlook on life

overwhelming majority

place a premium on

pressing need

pros and cons

recent developments

redeeming features

relative merits

room for improvement

secret of success

shining example

sigh of relief

sorry end

stress and strain

take full advantage

thriving business

time frame

to no avail

turning point

turn of events

unvarnished truth

vantage point

vast majority

viable alternative

well-rounded

with a vengeance

These expressions can be heard occasionally in oral discourse, when a speaker's velocity through his country of ideas makes him depend on familiar landmarks. Writing, however, provides time for greater precision and vitality in phrasing.

Clichés tend to be phrases rather than single words because several units, often alliterated *(soft as silk)*, are required to create the frozen predictability that makes them offensive. But a number of single words, worn out by overwork, can be thought of as small cousins to clichés: *approach, area, aspect, concept, facet, factor, feature, format, impact, level, phase, posture, problem, reaction, reflect, scenario, structure, thrust, typical.*

The rigidity that makes a reader's understanding of clichés and their cousins automatic can be seen in certain expressions that have become so locked together during centuries of repetition that their constituent elements are no longer recognizable. Many people would have difficulty defining *shrift, stead, fell, scot,* or *hue*; yet "short shrift," "stand in good stead," "one fell swoop," "scot-free," and "hue and cry" roll off the tongue or pen with thoughtless ease. (*Shrift* means confession—*short shrift* refers to the brief time a condemned prisoner had to confess prior to his execution; *stead* comes from Middle English *stede,* place; *fell* is a Middle English word meaning fierce, lethal, dire; *scot* means tax; *hue* is derived from Old French *huer,* to shout, which, combined with cry, became a legal term for the outcry that obligated all who heard it to join in the pursuit of a felon.)

But rigidity and repetition, while often flaws in writing, have another side. The instructor who insists that "a writer should never employ an expression he has heard before" has forgotten that language is possible only because of recurring patterns, that understanding is based on predictability, that good usage is a compromise between repetition and original-ity. The instructor who lands hard on clichés would be just as unhappy with original spellings, or objects put before verbs, or violated idioms: *in words other,* instead of *in other words*; *by example,* instead of *for example*; *to defer toward,* instead of *to defer to.* Clichés, then, are not wrong in any absolute sense. They simply fall outside the desired middle ground:

See **Slang, Jargon,** and **Variety.**

Coherence is a word perfectly explained by its Latin root, "to stick together," which describes the single most important feature of good prose. Other terms for this quality abound—unity, interrelatedness, consistency, focus, tight organization, logic, congruity—all of which express the notion that the parts of a composition need to be grouped appropriately. Nuts screw onto bolts, wheels turn on bearings, drive shafts tie into universal joints, and the entire construction rolls along in the same direction.

The principle of coherence applies at every level. The composition as a whole will be enhanced if the writer sticks to the main point throughout, an achievement usually accomplished by selecting the relevant subpoints and details and discarding the rest; by keeping the reader informed as to how each smaller proposition relates to the larger thesis; by taking up topics in an orderly sequence. Chronology provides a familiar form of order: Theodore Roosevelt campaigned in Cuba; he became governor of New York; he was elected vice-president; then McKinley was assassinated. Space as well as time can be organized by contiguity: first the gate, then the walk, next the steps, then the door. Cause and effect establishes a sequence understood by every reader: "If a man write a better book, preach a better sermon, or make a better mouse-trap than his neighbour . . . the world will make a beaten path to his door." The writer also needs to use internally compatible diction and to stick to the same opinion about the material, which is what instructors mean by consistent tone or attitude. And that opinion should come from a narrative voice, a writer's conception and presentation of himself (point of view, in technical terminology) that remains stable.

In the paragraph, coherence is achieved by concentrating on one element of the topic, or at least on one element at a time, and by keeping verb tenses consistent. In the sentence, subjects should be close to their verbs, modifiers should hold hands with what they modify. Don't write that "the nuclear power plant will not be built because of an unacceptable survey of geologic conditions" if the fault lies in the geology, not the survey. Often, small rearrangements can put the elements of a sentence in the relation to each other that will best express the author's meaning. "The proof was largely based on hearsay evidence" makes better sense if the *largely* is shifted: "The proof was based largely on hearsay evidence." A composition theorist tells us that "sonnets and notes to the plumber come equally within the purview of writing theory," but he should have written "notes to the plumber and sonnets" in order to shut off the bizarre possibility of sonnets to the plumber. UPI reports the following: "'If agreement is reached during the mediation period, it will of course have to be submitted to the various union memberships for ratification,' said Horvitz, flanked by three union presidents and Deputy Postmaster General James Conway, the government's top negotiator." But Horvitz, not Conway, was the government's top negotiator.

Coherence is often a matter of getting things in the right order. Here are some sentences with suggestions for improvement:

The policeman, after a lengthy chase involving four patrolmen and two squad cars, one of which was totally destroyed when it overturned and then burned, shot the burglar.

Put the subject and verb together: The *policeman shot* the burglar, after....

The two women have, for over twenty years, not been able to understand one another.

Relocate the *not* after *have*, to alert the reader to the negative force of the statement.

The judge awarded Mrs. Bellacose's husband a reasonable right of visitation.

Make it *a right of reasonable visitation*, since the right is absolute. It is the visits that must be reasonable.

Robert Henri felt like Whitman, that America was a land of artistic opportunity.

Change to: Robert Henri, like Whitman, felt that....

Tolstoy makes use of what Gérard Génette calls proleptic and analeptic techniques, that is, he goes arbitrarily into the past and future time of his tale.

The explanation of *proleptic* and *analeptic* won't help the reader unless the explanatory terms come in the same order as the original terms—proleptic (anticipating): analeptic (recovering) = future: past.

Coherence also demands internal consistency. Some examples:

Like Marcus Aurelius, I discovered that one should be careful what he sets his heart upon, for you will surely find it.

You should be changed to *he* for consistency.

> The directory will include information about persons who made hotel reservations in advance or sent their address to convention headquarters.

Change *address* to *addresses*, to agree with *persons*.

> Turning to the second issue, *Gibson's Suits in Chancery* sets forth certain guidelines concerning retroactive decrees.

State who is doing the turning, for it can not be *Gibson's Suits*: We now turn to the second issue, the retroactive decree, which is governed by *Gibson's Suits in Chancery*.

See **Ambiguity, Connection, Paragraphing, Thesis, Usage** ("only").

Conciseness.   The Lord's Prayer contains 54 words, the Ten Commandments 296 words, the Bill of Rights 462 words. The recent Report of the Commission on Federal Paperwork—which attacks the "unprecedented paperwork burden" and seeks to "minimize ... information reporting"—contains approximately 1,381,000 words, gathered compactly into 37 volumes.

The enemies of conciseness have many names—wordiness, pedantry, redundancy, pomposity, tautology—but these words all point to the same problem: two pounds of ideas in five pounds of prose. Such writing is inherently weak, since needless expressions smother significant ones. A writer can think of his sentence as an open boat riding low in the water, with only six inches of freeboard, three if the reader is dull-witted or inattentive. Even a small amount of unnecessary cargo slows the progress toward understanding; an excessive amount swamps the boat.

Some examples of cargo that should be jettisoned:

This case presents the question of the utilization of permits.	This case concerns the use of permits.
The University has taken a very favorable posture in relation to a new library.	The University favors a new library.
I heard a rumor to the effect that he died.	I heard a rumor that he died.
In conclusion it is my opinion that he did indeed lie.	I believe he lied.
They shared an apartment in common.	They shared an apartment.
The students engage in a group reading situation.	The students read together.
A new government study casts doubt on the value of home water filters in the area of pricing and effectiveness.	A new government study suggests that home water filters may be overpriced and ineffective.
It results from the foregoing reasons and an examination of all the facts and circumstances that this Court concludes the case is dismissed.	The case is dismissed.

Double expressions—saying the same thing twice—are in many cases built deeply into the language: *uprising; strait and narrow* (strait means narrow); *time and tide wait for no man* (tide originally meant time or season); *starve to death* (the Old English *steorfan* meant simply to die, and gradually became particularized, though *starve from cold* was still in use in the nineteenth century). Flagrant doubles should be avoided:

co-conspirators	not at all entirely certain	the one basic element
egress out of		
enclosed inside of	proceed forward	they mutually agreed
his own self-interest	prone on his stomach	two twins
new innovations	social societies	young juveniles

Other words and expressions can often be omitted to advantage:

as I have said	in terms of
as previously stated	interestingly enough
as we have seen	in the final analysis
definitely	it seems to me
for example	it should be noted that
for instance	needless to say (an expression that contains better advice than its user recognizes)
in a sense (a phrase that leaves the reader to figure out what sense the author intended)	
	not to mention (which means to mention)
indeed	
in fact	suffice it to say

A common kind of prolixity squanders the reader's time by telling him you are going to tell him something ("I will present an analysis in three steps") or by tracing how you went about it ("First I decided to investigate. . . . "). Unless you have a very elaborate and complex task, there is no need to discourse at length on your method. Feed your reader the cake, not the cookbook.

Conciseness should not be considered an attack on all forms of repetition. Prose without a certain amount of repetition is like a house so tightly insulated and sealed that the fireplace will not draw: writing and buildings require breathing room. But repetition can be distinguished from redundancy. Repetition is useful restatement, designed to achieve coherence, connection, interest; redundancy is unnecessary and dispensable restatement, which adds neither to meaning nor persuasion.

In the preceding discussion, the statement about breathing room repeats the house simile and furthers the reader's understanding. But the phrase "and dispensable" in the last sentence of the paragraph is redundant and should be omitted.

See **Jargon.**

Connection.   If coherence is the first principle of good prose (see earlier entry), connection is the second. To some extent the terms overlap, but coherence (Latin, "to stick together") can be thought of as a clumping of elements; connection ("to tie together") as the joining of clumps.

Connection thus refers to the bridges between sections, to the transitions (from *transire,* "to go across") from one section to another. These transitions, necessary within sentences, between sentences, and between paragraphs, are created in two ways. One is the use of conjunctions and other linking words and phrases: *also, although, and, because, but, finally, for example, however, if . . . then, in short, in the first place,*

nevertheless, on one hand . . . on the other, on the contrary, or,
secondly, similarly, specifically, therefore, thus. These words
are crucial in moving the reader from one point to the next,
but—like most techniques in writing—they need to be spiced
with variety. The skilled writer avoids leaning heavily on
overworked connectives: *as previously noted, for example,*
however, in conclusion, likewise, nevertheless.

The second method of transition employs the repetition of
key words and ideas in order to keep the reader's attention
focused on the topic as he or she moves along. And repetition
of less important words, often on the boundaries between
sections, helps to slide the reader from one section to the next.
These repetitions are achieved in various ways:

> The use of the same phrase (". . . led to extraordinary
> results. These results . . . .")

> Subtle turns of phrase (" 'We cannot,' he said, 'tell the
> whole life.' What could be told . . . .")

> Different phrasing for the same concept ("The applause
> was so loud Grant could not speak. This burst of
> noise . . . ."). Pronouns, of course, fit into this category.

These various techniques of repetition often employ parallel
grammatical structures.

See the example below and Parallelism.

The following quotation illustrates the effectiveness of well-
connected prose, especially when one deals with a complex set
of ideas. It is extracted from a decision in a complicated
squabble between the wife and the heirs of a man, McNeil,
who died shortly after his divorce hearing. The issue concerns

the precise time the divorce became effective, since the judge who granted the divorce also died, apparently before formally signing the decree. The "plaintiff" is the surviving, sometime divorced wife; *nunc pro tunc* ("now for then") refers to a retroactive legal decision.

The attorneys state that McNeil acquired additional property after the divorce hearing, and that he left a will. They further state that the court's ruling on the present motion will have a substantial effect upon the property rights of the plaintiff and McNeil's heirs. If the divorce decree is not entered, the plaintiff would take the real property as tenant by the entirety, would have widow's rights in the after-acquired property, and could dissent from the will. On the other hand, if the divorce decree is entered *nunc pro tunc,* the plaintiff would have a one-half undivided interest in the real property as a tenant in common, would have no interest in the after-acquired property, and could not affect the will.

Two questions are involved. First, can a successor judge enter a *nunc pro tunc* decree involving the action of a predecessor judge? Second, is this a proper case for the entry of a *nunc pro tunc* decree? The answer to both questions is yes.

The importance of the connections in this efficiently dispatched decision can be seen if they are highlighted:

The (attorneys) (state) that (McNeil) acquired additional property after the divorce hearing, and that (he) left a will. (They) (further state) that the court's ruling on the present motion will have a substantial effect upon the property rights of the plaintiff and McNeil's heirs. (If) the divorce decree is not entered, the plaintiff (would take) the real property as tenant by the entirety, (would have) widow's rights in the after-acquired property, and (could dissent) from the will. On the other hand, (if) the divorce decree is entered *nunc pro tunc,* the plaintiff (would have) a one-half undivided interest in the real property as a tenant in common, (would have) no interest in the after-acquired property, and (could not) affect the will.

(Two questions) are involved. (First,) can a (successor judge) enter a *nunc pro tunc* decree involving the action of a (predecessor judge)? (Second,) is this a proper case for the entry of a *nunc pro tunc* decree? The (answer) to (both questions) is yes.

Note also the repetition of key words: *property* (six times); *divorce, will,* and *nunc pro tunc* (three times each).

Dictionaries. Some writers can safely ignore rhetoric and grammar books and scoff at usage manuals, but no writer can dispense with a dictionary. There are three basic types:

HISTORICAL The standard work is the *Oxford English Dictionary (OED),* published in thirteen volumes in 1933. This dictionary, begun in the 1870s and first titled *A New English Dictionary on Historical Principles,* is outdated, but its chronologically arranged citations for each word make it a permanently valuable record of the thousand years of English that stretch from the death of King Alfred in 901 to that of Queen Victoria in 1901. A user can discover that our tame and grandmotherly word *nice* had a flaming youth, meaning "foolish" in 1290, "lascivious" in 1366, "extravagant" in 1430, "strange" in 1500, "delicate" in 1562, "shy" in 1634, "fastidious" in 1706, "dainty" in 1766, "precise" in 1784. These meanings and a dozen others are illustrated by extensive quotations—almost two hundred for *nice,* almost two million in the dictionary as a whole. All thirteen volumes of the *OED* are now available in a two-volume micrographic edition, which comes with a magnifying glass.

UNABRIDGED A family quarrel exists between the two best unabridged dictionaries. G. & C. Merriam's long-standard *Webster's New International Dictionary of the English Language,* 2nd ed., 1934, was challenged but not superseded by Merriam's *Third New International Dictionary* in 1961. This feisty youngster is based on principles of linguistics set down in the second quarter of the century which hold that language is made in the streets, not in the courts or academies; that speech has primacy over writing; and that a dictionary should describe language as it is used, not prescribe certain ways to use it. The *Third's* admission of *ain't* (but not *fuck*— that sturdy favorite did not appear in dictionaries until the late 1960s), its abandonment of most usage labels, and its flamboyant citations caused an uproar that still echoes in the once quiet halls of lexicography.

The difference between the two dictionaries is about what one might expect between a forty-five-year-old father and his eighteen-year-old son. The *Second's* entry for *go* includes quotations from Sir Philip Sidney, Shakespeare, Bunyan, Scott, Dr. Arbuthnot, and an old proverb: "Who goeth a borrowing goeth a sorrowing." The *Third* quotes from Dorothy Barclay, Huntington Hartford, *Newsweek,* Betty Smith ("don't ask for the bedpan during the night unless you really have to *go*"), and Gontran de Poncins ("it's that stink of caribou about them that I can't *go*"). Which dictionary will give you what you want depends on what you want from a dictionary.

COMPACT DESK OR COLLEGE EDITIONS   My choice, because it sails a middle course between description and prescription, is Houghton Mifflin's *American Heritage Dictionary of the English Language,* 1969. This dictionary of 155,000 entries (there are 550,000 in *Webster's Second*) has an excellent series of notes on usage derived from the democratic procedure of polling a usage panel of 118 members and citing their opinions in percentages. The panel, for example, disapproves of *I feel badly* by 61%, *enthuse* by 76%, *it is me* by 78% (although only 40% find it unacceptable in speech), *ain't* by 99%. As the near unanimity concerning *ain't* demonstrates, the American Heritage Usage Panel measures opinions about usage, rather than usage itself. And the opinions are those of a conservative group whose average age, at the time of publication, was sixty-four. Nevertheless, the group as a whole well represents current opinion concerning standards for formal writing. Other good desk dictionaries include *Webster's New World Dictionary of the American Language* (2nd ed., 1976), *The*

Random House College Dictionary (rev. ed., 1975), and *Webster's Collegiate Dictionary* (8th ed., 1973; based on the unabridged *Third*). Smaller paperback dictionaries are of limited usefulness.

Etymology, the study of word origins, provides an interesting and painless way to develop greater sensitivity to language and greater precision in its use. A remarkable world of word histories is as close as a dictionary—which, for any writer, should be about two feet. Many words come directly into English from other languages: *conspiracy* (Latin *conspirare,* literally "breathing together"), *hibachi* (Japanese, "fire-bowl"), *gung ho* (Chinese, "work together"), *tomahawk* (Algonquian *tamahaac,* "cutting tool"). Some memorialize historical events or people: *teddy bear,* from Teddy Roosevelt's hunting exploits; *sideburns,* from the style of side whiskers worn by Civil War General Ambrose Burnside. Often words and expressions continue on, under their own steam, after the era or occupation or object they refer to has changed. *By and large* was originally a nautical term: *by* meant that the sails were close-hauled, *large* that they were free. A ship that sailed well by and large did so under both conditions, thus generally, as the phrase means now. Sometimes a knowledge of etymology helps in remembering words. One is not likely to forget the meaning of *supercilious* once the Latin roots are discovered—"above the eyelid," hence "eyebrow." A raised eyebrow has indicated scorn since Roman times. While some words connect us to the past, others measure the distance. A history of religious beliefs could be written from the changes in the meanings of *panic* (fear of the Greek god Pan), *auspicious* ("to look at a bird" for divination), *disaster* ("ill-starred"), *enthusiasm* ("inspired by a god"), and *holiday* ("holy day").

Consider the following:

assassin	From Arabic *hashshāsh,* "hashish addict"
belittle	Coined by Jefferson in *Notes on the State of Virginia* (1782), the word was attacked as a barbarism by conservative British critics
debauch	French, "[to take one] away from work"
dilapidate	Latin, "to throw stones apart"
helpmate	A word derived at least in part from a series of typographical changes and mistakes. In the King James Bible of 1611, Genesis 2:18 was translated as "I will make an help meet for him," in which "meet" carried the Renaissance English meaning of "proper," "appropriate." The words "help meet" were later printed together as *helpmeet,* and then, since that made little sense, it was changed to *helpmate.* This slippage from the unknown to a suitable known word can be observed at first hand with any learner. American children often mistake *wheelbarrow* for *wheelbarrel,* or *marshmallow* for *marshmellow,* since *barrow* and *mallow* are relatively uncommon. Their elders, on the same principle, sometimes allow *sacrilegious* to slide to *sacreligious* or *Westminster* to *Westminister.*
hermaphrodite	A combination from the names of the Greek god Hermes and the goddess Aphrodite
jeep	From "G.P.," an abbreviation of "general-purpose" vehicle

lewd

From Old English *laewede,* "lay" (that is, not of the clergy). *Lewd* originally meant "unlettered," "ignorant" (Middle English poets liked the alliterative contrast of "the learned and the lewed") and has gone downhill from there.

This process of the meaning of a word changing for the worse, called pejoration, can also be seen in *silly* (originally "happy," "blessed"), *knave* (originally "youth"), and *egregious* (literally "standing out from the herd," which has slid from "distinguished" to "conspicuously bad"). Occasionally the process is reversed. *Pretty* is an upwardly mobile word that originally meant "cunning," "tricky." *Shrewd* comes from Middle English *schrewe,* "evil," "dangerous."

lynch

Lynch demonstrates that not all words can be definitively traced. Some dictionaries cite Charles Lynch (1736-96), a Virginia justice of the peace whose extralegal methods were directed against Tories; but the word is also linked with Captain William Lynch (1742-1820), another Virginian, who drew up a pact with his Pittsylvania County neighbors in 1780 to protect themselves from "great and intolerable losses by a set of lawless men." And another candidate is Lynche's Creek in South Carolina, the meeting place in 1768 of a band of anti-Tory "regulators."

maroon
From Spanish *cimarrón,* "fugitive slave," "wild"; originally either "living on the mountain tops" (*cima,* summit) or "living in the thicket" (*cimarra,* bushes)

nocent
"Guilty," the lost positive of "innocent," in use up to the seventeenth century. A number of similar words—*clement, couth, evitable, peccable, reck,* and *ruth*—are commonly employed only in their negated meanings: *inclement, uncouth, inevitable, impeccable, reckless, ruthless.*

O.K.
Probably first used to mean "all correct" in the Boston *Morning Post* in 1839 during an acronym epidemic; then reinvented and popularized by the O.K. Club, a political organization formed by Democrats to support Martin Van Buren's campaign for re-election in 1840. *O.K.* stood for Van Buren's nickname, "Old Kinderhook," from his birthplace—Kinderhook, New York. The slogan did better than Van Buren, who lost to Harrison.

stark naked
Naked all the way down, from the Old English *steort,* "tail"

taxi
Shortened form of *taximeter cab* (*cab* itself was shortened from *cabriolet* in the early nineteenth century). Other truncated words that have become established include *mob* from *mobile vulgus* (Latin, "fickle crowd"),

	bus from *omnibus* (the dative plural, "for all," of Latin *omnis*, "all"), and *squash* from *isquoutersquash* (Algonquian).
trivia	From Latin *tri* (three) *via* (road), crossroads; hence the common way, of little significance
whiskey	A word whose many transformations— *whiskybae, usquebaugh, uisce beathadh*— derive ultimately from Old Irish *uisce* (water) *bethad* (of life).

This sort of knowledge, fascinating in its own right, should be displayed lightly, for words often drift from their original moorings. Few writers today use *awful* to mean "full of awe" or *prevent* to mean "to come before." But the careful user of language will wish to distinguish between drifting and being cut loose entirely. "The atrocious conduct of a prison guard" is better usage than "an atrocious amount of salt on his dinner," since the root of *atrocious* means "cruel," "horrible." One might object that most modern users of the word don't know and don't need to know the Latin derivation. True enough, but a problem remains. Since the word has been employed for three centuries by speakers and writers with that knowledge, it has acquired a history, a set of secondary characteristics. The user who "pours an atrocious amount of salt" violates not just the etymology but the environment of usage, continuing to the present day, created by that etymology. Thus a knowledge of word origins can be of special importance to the modern writer who does not have mastery of the languages on which English is built.

And etymology opens the way to subtle effects. In discussing Clytemnestra, waiting for her husband to come home, waiting so she can murder him, a scholar neatly describes her as *sanguine,* calling up the meaning "optimistic" as well as the root *sanguineus,* "bloody." These two meanings, opposed in modern use, were once united in medieval physiology, which held that the dominance of one of the four fluids (humors) of the body—blood, phlegm, choler, black bile—determined an individual's character. This theory has left a rich linguistic heritage: *sanguine, phlegmatic, choleric, melancholy* (Greek for black bile), and *humor* itself, which has changed over the years from fluid to disposition to caprice to comicality.

Exceptions to the advice in this guide not only should be recognized and grudgingly tolerated, they should be encouraged. Composition teachers lecture their students about the virtues of a sentence that closes cleanly and rapidly, and then turn with joy to Faulkner's thousand-word sentences in "The Bear." Instructors preach unity in the series but praise Mark Twain's twist of the form: "the white people came, and brought trade, and commerce, and education, and complicated diseases, and civilization." Students are admonished to "keep a consistent point of view" and then told how, in the first chapter of *Madame Bovary,* Flaubert brilliantly establishes and then abandons the point of view of Charles's classmates at the lycée in Rouen. Students find "mixed metaphor" (or "mixed metaphor!") gleefully red-penciled in the margins of their papers, but somehow Shakespeare escapes criticism when Hamlet wonders if he should "take arms against a sea of troubles." Instructors warn against "absolute expressions" (see above, p. 1), yet revel in the blast of absolutism that Louis T. Milic fires at what is, in his opinion, the foe of literacy:

> Television should no more be protected by the First
> Amendment than bubonic plague or earthquakes. [It] must be
> destroyed.... Not simply turned off, but the sets, scripts, office
> furnishings, transmitters, masts and all piled up and burned in
> the middle of Sixth Avenue, the managers, vice-presidents,
> anchormen and assorted flacks and flunkies with their families
> relocated in Alaska, Utah, Wyoming and North Dakota, their
> buildings razed, the blocks sunk into the sea and salt spread
> over their foundations. That might perhaps take care of it.

These examples prove two points. All rules about writing
can be broken. The trick is knowing when, and here
imaginative writers—often used as models for teaching
composition—are not necessarily safe guides. Expert writers
can deviate from standard usage precisely because they have
swallowed it; they can work subtly with exceptions to the
normal because they have mastered the normal. The process
of reading, psycholinguists tell us, involves fulfilling expectations—lexical, syntactic, semantic. The reader uses the words,
structure, and meaning of a text at any given point to predict
what will follow. Imaginative literature often works in
calculated ways to upset these expectations. Try explaining
Emily Dickinson's grammar to a youngster or a foreign
student still struggling to understand word order, capitalization, punctuation, and the indefinite article:

> And then, in Sovereign Barns to dwell—
> And dream the Days away,
> The Grass so little has to do
> I wish I were a Hay—

Thus exceptions to the suggestions in this guide should be
encouraged, but with discretion. One must know the point
before one can deal in counterpoint.

False comparative.   "Executive Tax Service is tailored to meet the needs of persons with the more complex income tax returns"; "He was an engineer who seemed to be more conscious of the subtleties of technical language"; "The book is designed for younger readers." If no less complex returns, no less conscious engineer, no older readers are cited or suggested, then no comparison exists and the writer doesn't need the comparative form. Such false comparatives usually arise from the writer's belief that the comparison is implicit, a belief based on sound principles of language: much communication derives from assumptions shared in advance by writer and reader and from ideas suggested rather than stated in the text. Much of our understanding comes from reading, as the expression goes, between the lines. But when an implied comparison gets so tenuous that it works as a comparison only for the writer and not for the reader, it should be avoided.

Sometimes, of course, writers deliberately use the false comparative to insinuate information that would be rejected by common sense or countered by the opposition if stated explicitly. Raleigh Lights give "more satisfying tobacco flavor"; Kents have a "smoother, fuller taste"; Camels are made with a "richer-tasting blend." And deep in a shady glen beside a green pool, the cool hot girl vibrates with the information that "Salems smoke cooler." Cooler than what? R. J. Reynolds and Company hope that, distracted by girl and glen, we will fill in cooler than Luckies, Marlboros, perhaps even Kools—rather than grass fires, jet exhausts, and smelting furnaces.

Footnote and bibliographic forms follow certain conventions in formal writing that provide shortcuts for the writer and consistency for the reader. Footnotes indicate where you got your material, they relieve you of the responsibility for errors which may be in that material, and they allow your reader to reconstruct your argument. Use footnotes to identify a direct quotation; a statement of fact that is not common knowledge; charts, maps, tables, diagrams, and statistics; a summary or paraphrase of an author's opinion; any borrowed idea, opinion, or conclusion; and to insert additional comments, although one should resist the temptation.

Here are some common types of footnotes illustrating the basic form for books (1, 4, 6, 10) and periodicals (7); with examples of the form for a reprinted volume (1), a work cited in another work (3), a multivolume work (4), an edited book (6), a book with two authors (10), a second edition (10), and subsequent references (2, 5, 8, 9). In devising footnotes whose types are not illustrated here, remember that the goals are convenience for the reader and consistency of form, in that order.

[1]Oliver Elton, *Dickens and Thackeray* (1924; rpt. New York: Haskell House, 1970), p. 47.

[2]Elton, p. 47.

[3]William M. Thackeray, "A Shabby Genteel Story," *Fraser's Magazine* (1840); cited in Elton, p. 76.

[4]John Forster, *The Life of Charles Dickens* (London: Chapman & Hall, 1872-74), II, 65.

[5]Forster, III, 197.

[6]Charles Dickens, *Letters to Charles Lever,* ed. F. V. Livingston (Cambridge, Mass.: Harvard University Press, 1933), pp. 218-20.

[7]Alice Meynell, "Charles Dickens as a Man of Letters," *Atlantic Monthly,* 46 (January 1903), 54.

[8]Elton, *Dickens and Thackeray,* p. 204.
    or
[8]Elton, p. 204.

[9]Meynell, "Charles Dickens," p. 56.
    or
[9]Meynell, p. 56.

[10]John Butt and Kathleen Tillotson, *Dickens at Work,*
2nd ed. (London: Methuen, 1957), p. 258.

Once you have mastered the rules of footnoting, the next
step is to learn how to break them. Collective footnotes,
summary footnotes, and references in the text should be used
to keep the number of footnotes—and the appearance of
pedantry—to a minimum. Information stated in the text (an
author's name, for example) need not be repeated in a note.
Often a series of references or quotations can be reduced to a
single footnote ("the factual information contained in the
introduction was derived from . . . ."; "the quotations in the
following pages are all from . . . ."). Once you have given a full
citation in a note, succeeding citations may be given
parenthetically in the text: (*Dombey and Son,* p. 125), or
(*Dombey,* p. 125), or just (p. 125) if the reference is clear.
    If you wish to make things easy for your reader (and if you
are writing a work that will be microfilmed), place footnotes
at the foot of the page, not at the end of the paper.

Bibliographies repeat the information given in footnotes,
but in slightly different form:

Butt, John, and Kathleen Tillotson. *Dickens at Work.* 2nd ed.
    London: Methuen, 1957.

Dickens, Charles. *Letters to Charles Lever.* Ed. F. V.

Livingston. Cambridge, Mass.: Harvard University Press, 1933.

——. *The Mystery of Edwin Drood.* Boston: Fields, Osgood & Co., 1870.

Elton, Oliver. *Dickens and Thackeray.* 1924; rpt. New York: Haskell House, 1970.

Forster, John. *The Life of Charles Dickens.* 3 vols. London: Chapman & Hall, 1872-74.

Meynell, Alice. "Charles Dickens as a Man of Letters." *Atlantic Monthly,* 46 (January 1903), 52-59.

New York Times, 14 April 1870, pp. 17, 19.

A bibliography is not necessary with a short essay, unless the writer wishes to insert information in addition to that contained in the footnotes ("Sources Consulted," perhaps, as well as "Sources Cited"). The best bibliographies are annotated.

Common abbreviations used in footnotes and bibliographies:

abr.	abridged, abridgment	ed(s).	editor(s), edited by, edition
bk(s).	book(s)		
c. or ca.	about (refers to time)	e.g.	for example
		enl.	enlarged
cf.	compare	et al.	and others
ch(s).	chapter(s)	ibid.	the same
col(s).	column(s)	i.e.	that is

l(l).	line(s)		n.p.	no place (of publication)
ms(s)	manuscript(s) (MS. when referring to a specific ms)		p(p).	page(s)
			rev.	revised, revision
n(n).	note(s), footnote(s)		rpt.	reprinted, reprint
n.d.	no date		trans.	translated, translation
no(s).	number(s)		vol(s).	volume(s)

Op. cit., loc. cit., supra, infra, and *v.* are, fortunately, no longer commonly used in scholarly writing. Even *ibid.* is to be avoided, according to the new *MLA Handbook.* The abbreviations given in the list above are appropriate in footnotes and bibliographies, but avoid using them—especially *i.e.* and *e.g.*—in your text. In general, use abbreviations sparingly in formal prose. Nineteenth century is preferable to 19th century. When using an abbreviation a number of times in succession, spell it out in full the first time with the abbreviation in parentheses: National Labor Relations Board (N.L.R.B.); then use only the shortened form.

For additional information on footnote and bibliographic form in the humanities see the *MLA Handbook for Writers of Research Papers, Theses, and Dissertations* (New York: Modern Language Association of America, 1977). For style manuals in other fields, see the *MLA Handbook,* pp. 94-96. In technical and scientific fields, footnotes are usually omitted in favor of brief parenthetical references in the text (Labov, 1969, 23-25) that are keyed to a bibliography. Legal writers give full information the first time a case is mentioned—*Ada Resources, Inc. v. Don Chamblin & Assoc., Inc.,* 361 So.2d 1339 (La. App. 1978)—and abbreviate later references (*Ada v. Chamblin,* 1342).

Form and content should be coordinated whenever possible, so that the writer's structure supports the ideas in a sentence, just as an actor's gestures support his words. This coordination is sometimes thought of as a special province of poetry, as in Herbert's "Easter Wings," in which the stanzas are shaped like wings; or in the dying Hamlet's request to Horatio, in which the trippingly Latinate first line contrasts with the heavy monosyllables of the second:

> Absent thee from felicity awhile,
> And in this harsh world draw thy breath in pain,
> To tell my story.

Prose writers also stay alert for opportunities for coordination, less spectacular perhaps in ordinary exposition than in poetry, although just as important: "Despite the extravagance of Poe's frightening plunges into the abysses of passion and guilt, we can understand them in our own small ways." Here the modest phrasing of "our own small ways," set against the arabesque "abysses of passion and guilt," brings Poe's meaning back from murder and uxoricide and applies it to a fireside quarrel.

One way to take advantage of structure is to put important statements and key phrases where the reader's attention is greatest: titles and beginnings—because, as organizing impressions, they govern the reader's expectations of what is to come; endings—because they linger in the memory as the most recent summarizing impressions. A skilled writer often maneuvers the final sentence to emphasize a crucial point or event:

> We were alone with the quiet day, and his little heart, dispossessed, had stopped.
>
> (Henry James, *The Turn of the Screw*)

See **Parallelism** for a special instance of the coordination of form and content.

Grammar, usage, and style. These related but distinguishable terms convey different meanings to different persons. Grammar taught in the schools differs from grammar defined by linguists, and linguists of various persuasions—transformational-generative, stratificational, tagmemic—quarrel among themselves. Usage in conservative quarters is a question of correctness, of unchanging right and wrong. Others see usage as a matter of appropriateness, which changes with the historical moment and the needs of individual writers. Some critics define style as the fusion of form and content, the indivisible wedding of how a statement is made with what it means. Their opponents insist that style has significance only if it refers to form as distinguished from content. These three debates are not easily resolved: many of the arguments about grammar stem from different premises; some recent battles in the usage war have been won by the relativists, but the notion of correctness dies hard; the truth in the form and content dispute probably lies in the middle. And the debates concern not only the meanings of these terms, but their relationships as well. Many linguists now limit their discussions of grammar to the basic principles and structure of the English language. Traditionalists, however, tend to include customs of usage in their definition of grammar. These relationships can be roughly diagramed as follows:

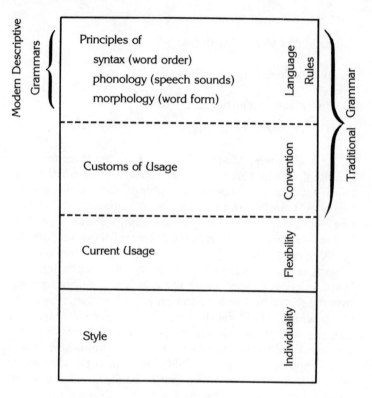

GRAMMAR refers to principles of language deeply embedded in fifteen hundred years of English. The subject-verb-object order of the normal English sentence provides a useful illustration. Old English, like Latin and Modern French and German, was an inflected language. That is, the forms of words signaled their functions in a sentence. Thus, two sentences with many similar words in Modern English:

The man waited for the horses.

The horses waited for the man.

are quite different in Old English:

Sē wer bād þaēm horsum.

þā hors bidon þaēm were.

In these sentences, Modern English "the" has three forms in Old English, *sē*, *þaēm*, and *þā*, depending on whether the noun modified is singular or plural, subject or object. Similarly "man" has the forms *wer* and *were* in the Old English; "horses" is *horsum* and *hors*; and the verb "waited" is *bad* in one instance, *bidon* in the other. Inflections reduce the need for rigid word order: *Sē wer* would mean "the man" as subject, no matter where it occurred in the sentence. But with fewer inflections, word order becomes crucial: interchanging "man" and "horses" in the Modern English sentences reverses the meaning. Old English was, in fact, a word-order language as well as an inflected language, but as inflections were lost—and the history of English is one of diminishing inflection—opportunities for flexibility in word order decreased. Subject-verb-object is now a law in English, and it is a law observed by all users. One may say "I don't have any" or "I ain't got none," but the deep grammatical structure of the two statements is the same. A truly ungrammatical sentence would be "Have any I don't," or "Ain't none got I."

USAGE is another matter, as can be seen in the concept of the double negative. In Old (500-1100) and Middle (1100-1400) English, the more negatives a writer used the more negative his meaning. In a Middle English text of *Sir Orfeo*, dated about 1330, a hunting party rides by without taking any game and then mysteriously disappears, leaving Orfeo to wonder where they went. The anonymous poet, piling up first a double and then a triple negative, puts it this way:

> Ac no best þai no nome
> No neuer he nist whider þai bi-come.
>
> [But no beast they not seized,
> Nor never he notknew whither they went.]

The eighteenth century attempted to impose law and order on English, and from that period we derive our rules about *lie* and *lay, it is I, between* and *among, shall* and *will,* and the double negative. In 1762 Robert Lowth, in his *Short Introduction to English Grammar,* first set out the precept, based on a dubious analogy to mathematics, that is still taught in our schools: "Two Negatives in English destroy one another, or are equivalent to an Affirmative." But in spite of two centuries of schoolmasters the double negative still flourishes among many speakers. And its use is not necessarily limited to the uneducated. When FAA administrator Langhorne Bond was asked if pilots were prepared to fly the DC-10 with one engine missing, he turned to a string of negatives capped by a double:

> No aircraft has ever been in the air under that circumstance. There is no pilot training for that eventuality. There are no procedures, no training, no nothing that a crew would go through or we could simulate.

The history of the double negative in English demonstrates that usage is often based on social force rather than linguistic principle, on convention rather than logic. As J. J. Lamberts points out, the notion that two negatives cancel one another doesn't hold even in mathematics: $-a + -a = -2a$. Nevertheless, the injunction against the double negative in serious writing has become fixed by the expansion of education in the nineteenth and twentieth centuries. Even though modern language study has shown the arbitrariness of many of our inherited rules, we are stuck with them.

Usage thus refers to what is currently acceptable in a language community. Here greater latitude exists than with grammar. There are differing language communities in the United States with differing purposes, audiences, and levels of formality for different acts of communication. Still, broad areas of agreement can be defined for a general language community made up of educated persons, professionals, editors, writers, teachers. *Ain't* is out, *finalize* is marginal, *O.K.* is acceptable in speech but it ain't O.K. in writing. These areas of agreement on usage, along with principles of grammar, help define what sociolinguist Peter Trudgill calls "Standard English": "that variety of English which is usually used in print, and which is normally taught in schools and to non-native speakers learning the language." Standard English is not inherently more correct, or beautiful, or logical, or expressive than non-standard dialects. But sanctioned by the society's educational, political, and economic institutions, Standard English is, quite simply, the language of power.

STYLE   embodies the voice of the author—the characteristics, attitudes, habits, and tricks that glimmer through his words and the way he puts them together. Grammar thus echoes across the centuries; usage is located specifically in time and place; style is personal and individual. Almost any sentence can be seen from these three points of view:

> If a man walk in the woods for love of them half of each day, he
> is in danger of being regarded as a loafer; but if he spends his

whole day as a speculator, shearing off those woods and making earth bald before her time, he is esteemed an industrious and enterprising citizen.

The grammar here is conventional and familiar—subjects precede verbs, prepositions govern phrases, adjectives modify nouns, independent but related clauses are separated by a semicolon. The writer seems fastidious about the subjunctive ("if a man walk"), but he immediately drops it in the following parallel clause ("if he spends"), and here grammar becomes subtly tuned. The switch from subjunctive to indicative suggests that walking in the woods for love is unlikely, hypothetical, contrary to fact; timbering, on the other hand, represents the normal, probable, inevitable course of human activity. The usage reveals a writer comfortable with a long, complexly but carefully organized sentence divided into parallel clauses (if...then; but if...then) that suggest nineteenth-century oratory, and we are not surprised to discover that the sentence was part of a lecture given in 1854. The style, with its clauses balanced to point up the contrast of walker and speculator, with the sharp bite of shearing next to the amiable joke about the balding earth, with its subversion of the quintessentially American gospel of industry and enterprise, points specifically to the genial yet astringent irony of Henry David Thoreau.

See **Usage.**

Handbooks on composition and rhetoric and dictionaries of usage exist by the dozens. Several of the best are listed below.

HANDBOOKS:

Frederick Crews. *The Random House Handbook.* 3rd ed. New York: Random House, 1980.

William Strunk, Jr., and E. B. White. *The Elements of Style.*
3rd ed. New York: Macmillan, 1979.

DICTIONARIES OF USAGE:

Bergen and Cornelia Evans. *A Dictionary of Contemporary
American Usage.* New York: Random House, 1957.

Wilson Follett. *Modern American Usage: A Guide.* Ed.
Jacques Barzun. New York: Hill and Wang, 1966.

Henry W. Fowler. *A Dictionary of Modern English Usage.*
2nd ed., rev. Ernest Gowers. New York: Oxford University
Press, 1965. Fowler's *Dictionary* of British (not American)
usage, originally published in 1926, is long out of date, but
it remains a curmudgeonly classic.

Margaret Nicholson. *A Dictionary of American-English
Usage Based on Fowler's "Modern English Usage."* New
York: Oxford University Press, 1957.

Robert C. Pooley. *The Teaching of English Usage.* Urbana, Ill.:
National Council of Teachers of English, 1974. Pooley's
comprehensive historical survey leads him to conclude that
"usage is the matter of becoming aware of choices in a large
number of specific instances. The English language is full of
possible variations. The term 'good usage' implies success in
making choices in these variations such that the smallest
number of persons...are distracted by the choices."

Students interested in the history and development of
English might wish to read Albert C. Baugh and Thomas
Cable's *History of the English Language* (3rd ed., 1978),
perhaps supplemented by H. L. Mencken's *The American Language* (1919-48). Jean Aitchison's *The Articulate Mammal*
(1976) provides an introduction to linguistics, psycholin-
guistics, and theories of modern grammar that is unusually

readable—a rare virtue in the writing of linguists. Teachers who care to investigate theories of composition should consult *The Philosophy of Composition* (1977), by E. D. Hirsch, Jr. Those faced with the rigors of teaching what is now called basic writing will need Mina P. Shaughnessy's *Errors and Expectations* (1977).

Homonyms (words that sound alike) are not synonyms. The following words should be differentiated:

affect (to influence)	effect (noun: result, influence) (verb: to bring about)
allusion (indirect reference)	illusion (false impression)
altar (church platform)	alter (to change)
capital (wealth, city, letter, chief)	capitol (building in which a legislature meets)
complement (that which completes)	compliment (praise)
conscious (aware, awake)	conscience (what keeps one morally awake)
continually (recurring)	continuously (unceasing)
council (assembly)	counsel (advice; advise) consul (foreign-service officer)
credible (believable)	credulous (gullible)
eminent (prominent)	imminent (impending) immanent (inherent)
flaunt (to show off)	flout (to show disrespect for)
hangar (for airplanes)	hanger (for clothes)

nauseous (causing nausea)	nauseated (suffering from nausea)
precede (to come before)	proceed (to go forward)
prescribe (to order, recommend)	proscribe (to condemn, forbid)
principal (chief)	principle (rule)
sensual (pertaining to the physical senses; often suggests sexuality)	sensuous (pertaining to the senses in general; can include the aesthetic)
subtlety (a noun)	subtly (an adverb)

Jargon, the special language of a specific group, occasionally begins with precise technical terms, such as "parameter" from mathematics or "interface" from hydrostatics, which, as they become generalized, tend to be used with monotonous frequency and ham-fisted inappropriateness by insiders and outsiders alike. Or it can be created instantly by torturing normal words and expressions: an educational administrator designs a program with a goal of "inservicing the principals." Either way, jargon is graceless and tiresome.

Jargon exists all around us—wherever there are language communities. Engineers talk of "preplanning" and "design phases"; generals have apparently invented "self-destruct" and the notorious "protective reaction strike"; real estate developers create "environmental habitats"; lawyers rely on "whereas," "hereinabove," "witnesseth," "the said case," "the party of the first part"; jailers work at "detention facilities"; computer programmers have given us "input" and "feedback"; fired government officials invariably return to "the private sector"; literary critics point to "the almost unbearable tension of ironic ambiguities"; educators talk of "hands-on learning experience"; academicians sprinkle their observations with "ontological" and "epistemological," "diachronic" and "synchronic," "microstructure" and "macroproposition," recalling Melville's observation that "the smatterer in science thinks that by mouthing hard words he understands hard things"; sociologists enjoy using "domestic infrastructure" when they mean family; economists lean to "tax shelter," "short-fall," "double-digit inflation"; a businessman reports on small dictating machines with "an in-house study of ultraslim word-processing equipment"; the author of an algebra textbook multiplies the difficulties with his explanation: "A numerical expression is a name for a number. The number is called the value of the expression. Whenever you replace a numerical expression with the simplest, or most common, name of its value, you say that you have simplified the expression."

The convoluted testimony in a recent breach-of-contract case inspired Tennessee Chancellor Robert Brandt to deliver a broadside from the bench at university jargoneers:

> The [Vanderbilt] Graduate School of Management devised its own language to substitute for words more commonly used. While it may be in vogue in academic programs, the jargon is new to this court. An area of study is called a "stem." A class is a "module." The "Resource Information Center" is what is usually known as a library. To the faculty, the "external environment" is the world outside the Graduate School of Management.

Vanderbilt might reply that judges and lawyers, in their attempt to elaborate precisely all possible contingencies, sometimes create a prose that seems to be the offspring of a marriage between jargon and prolixity:

> As collateral security for the payment of the indebtedness of the undersigned hereunder and all other indebtedness or liabilities of the undersigned to the bank, whether joint, several, absolute,

contingent, secured, unsecured, matured or unmatured, under
any present or future note or contract or agreement with the
bank (all such indebtedness and liabilities being hereinafter
collectively called the "obligations"), the bank shall have, and is
hereby granted, a security interest.

Englished from the original, as Renaissance translators used
to say, that statement means "I give the bank a security
interest on this debt and all other debts to the bank."

But someone else's jargon is easier to recognize than one's
own. Language specialists are as guilty as writers in other
fields, as can be seen from the following statement presented
at a recent Modern Language Association meeting concerned
with writing theory:

As I see it, basic writing theory will study two kinds of
phenomena. One kind pertains to structures of mature
discourse competence, the other to the developmental
sequence traversed by learners in acceding to mature
competence. The first implies investigation of the product of
learning, the second research on the process of its acquisition.
More specifically, inquiry into discourse competence will aim to
develop a system and a nomenclature (i.e., a theory)
characterizing the ideational structure of discourse—its
semantic connectedness, so to speak—in hierarchical ways that
bridge the large and almost totally uncharted gap between the
level whereon intra-propositional word-to-word relations are
studied by the generative semanticist, and the whole-discourse
level whereon the rhetorician classifies separate discourse
types.

Some of the expressions in these examples—"resource
information center," "security interest," "discourse competence"—point to a construction that deserves separate

discussion. Like necktie widths, jargon follows the fashions. One currently fashionable construction employs nouns to modify other nouns: *learning experience, demonstration model, job opportunity, power structure, object lesson, content enrichment program.* For the most part, there is nothing wrong with the use of the noun modifier, and it has a distinguished patrimony in Old English kennings: "sea-farer" for ship; "whale-road" for ocean. These expressions are related to a large tribe of double nouns, usually short, that have become single words: *necktie, mailman, pathway, farmhouse, wallpaper, wheelchair, woodpecker.* The problem with current usage seems to be located not in the idea of the noun-noun construction itself, but in its abuse. If a writer creates these expressions from long Latinate words, or from vague and general words, or allows them to swell from doubles to triples, then the ear protests and the mind rebels: *weather situation, value judgment, verification process, role model, activities resource person, education improvement experience, executive training workshop session.*

Since jargon commonly escapes from its specialized communities and infects the population at large, see **Clichés.** Compare **Slang.**

Latinisms. About half of our English vocabulary comes, directly or indirectly, from Latin—much more than from Old English, the Germanic parent of modern-day English, which was spoken in England from about 500 to 1100. Nevertheless, the working words—*man, wife, house, food, sun, stone, water, live, eat, talk, go, have, be*—as well as the rhythm and character of our language are English rather than Latin. Consider the following sentence: "Subsequent to the trial, the case was remanded for consideration of the pretermitted assignments of error which question the preponderance of the evidence, the corroboration of the defendant's identification, and the sufficiency of proof of the alleged donations." While perfectly correct, such heavily Latinate prose takes longer to comprehend than the shorter rhythms and sharper accents to which our English ears are tuned. "Subsequent" takes a millisecond longer to process than "after." If you smell smoke, "Fire!" will get you help quicker than "Conflagration!"

As a result of the four centuries of trilingualism that followed the victory of William of Normandy* over the British at Hastings in 1066, we often have a choice among synonyms with English, French, or Latin roots:

ENGLISH	FRENCH	LATIN
ask	question	interrogate
beat	vanquish	subjugate
climb	mount	ascend
fear	terror	trepidation
holy	sacred	consecrated
kill	destroy	exterminate

The English word tends to be shorter and more often used in speech. It is not, of course, necessarily more precise or effective, for the rich treasures of Latin vocabulary have substantially expanded the Old English word hoard. The issue comes down to appropriateness and to percentages. Strong twentieth-century English prose leans toward Germanic roots; it uses a Latinate vocabulary with discretion; it mixes long words with short; it avoids gratuitous polysyllabic sesquipedalianism.

Two smaller abuses of Latin deserve comment. A silly habit that seems to be on the increase sprinkles English unneces-

*The offspring of a liaison between the Duke of Normandy and a tanner's daughter, William illustrates how language follows the course of history. Before the battle he was known as "William the Bastard." After his triumph he became "William the Conqueror."

sarily with Latin prepositions: "it came down to labor *versus* management"; "he was *anti* big business"; "she traveled *via* plane." Another kind of half-breed Latin can be found in the legal community: "In the case *sub judice,* Thomas Fletcher *et ux*. had driven to the *situs* in a 1980 Chevrolet." [In the case under consideration, Thomas Fletcher and his wife had driven to the site in a 1980 Chevrolet.]

Literary writing and expository writing. The term "literary" can be used both as praise ("he is gifted with a literary style") and condemnation ("the essay is overly literary")—a complex fact which suggests that we need to differentiate between the ordinary workday character of expository prose and the special case of literary or creative or belletristic writing. A distinction seems particularly necessary since many writing instructors cull their examples and derive their methods of teaching exposition from literary texts. This longstanding practice can be justified in part, for the two forms overlap extensively, as indicated in the following diagram:

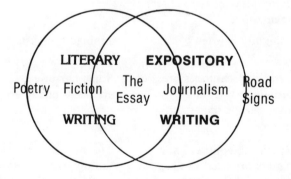

All writing attempts to convey a meaning, whose source is in the interaction between text and reader; all writing requires readers who are active, flexible, purposeful; all writing profits from the virtues described in this guide—coherence, connection, precision, conciseness, appropriateness of form, variety, specificity.

Yet there are many differences between expository writing and literary writing, expecially at the extremes. Expository writing leans toward the informative, the utilitarian, the denotative. Literary writing is, of course, instructive and useful, but it achieves its effects through the experiential, the aesthetic, the connotative. Some of these differences are suggested below:

LITERARY WRITING	EXPOSITORY WRITING
Patterns are often established and then broken. The literary text is less certain than the expository text, more open, more indeterminate, leaving play for the reader's imagination.	Predictable patterns—expectations—of meaning and form are firmly set up and rapidly fulfilled.
Ambiguity is often a virtue.	Ambiguity is usually a fault.
Narrative techniques are normally relied on—story, setting, character, imagery.	Some narrative techniques are occasionally employed.
Repetition, contrast, and imagery are used to keep elements of the surface text (the literal phrasing) in the reader's memory.	The surface text decays rapidly; the expository work is, on the whole, less rememberable than literary composition.

Rereading is rewarded, since textual meaning is often multiple, complex, and cannot be exhausted in one reading.	Rereading is often unnecessary, since meaning tends to be single, paraphrasable, grasped in one reading.

In actual texts, these differences are shadings rather than sharp distinctions. Many of our successful writers—Samuel Johnson and Charles Lamb to cite traditional examples; or, in the mid-twentieth century, George Orwell and E. B. White; or, currently, Lewis Thomas and John McPhee—derive their successes from a carefully cultivated middle ground between exposition and literature.

Metaphor. If it is true, as psychologists tell us, that the mind works by comparing and contrasting, by matching new impressions against stored experience, then it follows that metaphor is not a literary frill but a vital process that energizes the main pathways of human cognition. Words themselves are often metaphors, with their literal meanings half-submerged. Consider the component parts of *ghostwrite*, or *jitterbug*, or *goosestep*, or *jaywalk*. Even those people who object to metaphor—"flowery writing" they call it, using a metaphor— find themselves *keeping a sharp eye out,* or *making a deadline,* or *getting the inside track.* Comparative language is especially common, and especially useful, in giving the force of concrete reality to abstract things. We *grasp an idea, frame an argument, push a cause, handle a problem, block an objection, rest a case.* Metaphor surrounds us, embedded in advertising ("Merit smashes taste barrier"); in popular culture ("faster than a speeding bullet"); in folk wisdom and proverbial sayings ("a stitch in time saves nine"); in clichés ("smooth as glass"), which are often good similes fallen on evil days.

Successful metaphors—and similes, allusions, analogies, parables, and other comparisons—convey meaning with exactly those virtues recommended in this guide—conciseness, precision, variety, specificity. A housewife says it all when she describes herself as "hipdeep in children." A description of a liberal arts education as "a key to a box containing other keys" captures the immediate vocational disadvantages and the long-range lifetime advantages of such an education without the usual tiresome paragraphs that make commencement speeches laborious, sweaty affairs. David M. Potter, in arguing for a synthesis of history with psychology, sociology, and anthropology, turns to metaphor to cinch his argument:

> Though behavioral scientists may use the culture to explain human behavior, they must rely upon history to explain the culture. Although the practitioners of this oldest and these newest of disciplines may not be very congenial academic teammates, the fact remains that, if they are ever to scale the heights on which they hope to find a science of man, they must go roped together like other mountaineers.

An apt comparison seems to stick, which is perhaps why the *Oxford Dictionary of Quotations* and similar books can be read as anthologies of metaphor. Comparisons from such brilliantly metaphorical works as *Hamlet (soul of wit, primrose path, the mind's eye)* and the Bible *(hiding light under a bushel, new wine in old bottles, the blind leading the blind)* have been so thoroughly absorbed into the language they are used by millions who are unaware of the original sources. And metaphor is employed by the most diverse writers. Mark Twain fixed his jumping frog in the world's literature when he described, in Simon Wheeler's vernacular, the frog's attempt to hop with a belly full of buckshot:

> Dan'l give a heave, and hysted up his shoulders—so—like a Frenchman, but it warn't no use—he couldn't budge; he was

planted as solid as a church, and he couldn't no more stir than if he was anchored out.

Henry James never wrote about frogs, but he too depended on metaphor, which has the special virtue for James of bringing his abstruse style back to earth. Here is James on the difficulty of writing in Venice, where he was constantly drawn to his windows

> in the fruitless fidget of composition, as if to see whether, out in the blue channel, the ship of some right suggestion, of some better phrase, of the next happy twist of my subject, the next true touch for my canvas, mightn't come into sight. But I recall vividly enough that the response most elicited, in general, to these restless appeals was the rather grim admonition that romantic and historic sites, such as the land of Italy abounds in, offer the artist a questionable aid to concentration when they themselves are not to be the subject of it. They are too rich in their own life and too charged with their own meanings merely to help him out with a lame phrase; they draw him away from his small question to their own greater ones; so that, after a little, he feels, while thus yearning toward them in his difficulty, as if he were asking an army of glorious veterans to help him to arrest a peddler who has given him the wrong change.

Most books on writing include a stern admonition about avoiding mixed metaphors, and they cite some particularly outrageous examples: "The local bank bit off more than it could chew by engaging in cutthroat competition with the giants of finance." Perhaps that is why fledgling writers are afraid to try. And sports pages don't inspire confidence in the technique. Teams never win games or beat opponents, they crush, slaughter, maim, outgun, or squeak by the opposition. But we should worry more about writers forsaking the rich possibilities of comparative language than about mixed or abused metaphors. Many of our most skillful writers proceed rapidly from one idea to the next, skirting the edge of incongruous combinations. In the passages just quoted, Mark Twain jumps from church to ocean; Henry James moves in adjacent phrases from the ship of suggestion to the twist of the subject to the touch of the canvas. To be sure, obviously mixed or clumsy metaphors should be avoided, but don't let that inhibit you. A good writer takes risks. As a Navy pilot once put it, "No guts: no air medal."

Neologism, literally "new word," is a term used to praise Gerard Manley Hopkins when he coins a new expression ("worlds of wanwood leafmeal lie") and to damn the Charlottesville *Daily Progress* when they try it: "Health-wise, the cattle are not a threat." The first is a striking invention; the second merely tacks on a stereotyped suffix. "Wise" can be thought of as a destructive parasite, which fastens on the ends of nouns and sucks their vitality: *accidentwise, beautywise, investmentwise, schedulewise, taxwise.* A related species, "ize," transmogrifies adjectives and nouns into verbs: *concretize, finalize, normalize, prioritize, sermonize, youthfulize.* "Type" works the same way, attacking from the rear: *a business type, character type.* "An innovative type of program" is preferable to the slangy "an innovative type program," but both are far inferior to simply "an innovative program." Many American businessmen revel in such neologisms as "Smitty's Lumberteria," in Alexandria, Virginia. Perhaps Smitty provided the materials for a Washington, D.C. house described by its builder as "ultra-luxe." And then there are *kitchenettes* and *launderettes* and *superettes* (literally *largesmalls*). Next we will have *minisuperettes* and then *maximini-superettes* and finally, perhaps, *stores.*

Some pundits claim that "wise" and "ize" are peculiarly modern expressions that reveal the degenerate language practiced in the White House, the Pentagon, the conference room, the editorial office. This charge seems excessive.

Otherwise, in its original form—*on oþre wisan,* "in other manner"—was in use in England in the ninth century. *Baptize,* the first "ize" word in English, appeared in 1382; *organize* in 1413; *memorize* in 1519. Time seems to be the measure of respectability. These suffixes, then, are not always deleterious, but they are likely to distort the shape of perfectly good words when added on carelessly, needlessly. *Clockwise* serves a purpose; *timewise* does not.

See Jargon and Slang.

Numbers that can be expressed in one or two words in nontechnical prose are written in words (ten, ninety-nine, one hundred, 101, 999, one thousand, 1,001), unless there are a lot of numbers in a passage, in which case Arabic numerals should be used throughout. In showing a range of consecutive numbers over ninety-nine, abbreviate the second figure when it is within the same hundred: 95-98; 95-104; 288-89; 288-301; 1397-99; 1397-1401. (Note that consecutive numbers take a hyphen: 17-21; non consecutive numbers are listed individually: 17, 21.)

Obvious statements. Don't waste your time and your reader's by asserting that "the Civil War affected many Southern institutions" or that "Chief Justice Marshall, after his death in 1835, was not able to continue his interpretation of the Constitution," or that "any other matters that have not been presented to the Court will be decided when they are presented." Take the obvious for granted; explain the arcane.

Introductory remarks sometimes come under the heading of obvious statements, and many works would be stronger if first paragraphs, first sections, first chapters were condensed or omitted entirely. Many writers seem to need a running start which churns up a good deal of froth, like a goose taking off.

These introductory thrashings should be scrutinized for possible revision or deletion after the work is finished.

Obvious labels should be scrutinized also. Expressions like "for example," "in conclusion," and "ironically" are often unnecessary. Build your examples in, rather than thrusting them at your reader. If your paper is written so that it merely sputters out inconclusively on the last page, starting the final paragraph with "in conclusion" won't help. If you have an ironic statement, line up the elements so the irony shows and leave off the label: "There's a rule saying I have to ground anyone who's crazy [but] there's a catch, catch-22. Anyone who wants to get out of combat duty isn't really crazy." If Joseph Heller had written "but ironically there's a catch" he would have blunted the edge of Doc Daneeka's classic statement.

But see **Connection** to make certain your writing moves the reader from one section to the next. Obvious labels are cumbersome but, like crutches and wheelchairs, they may be useful at times to help you get around.

Paragraphing. The only formal unit of organization between the sentence and the entire composition is the paragraph. Normally it should have a single clear topic that, on one hand, supports the larger work, and on the other, is itself subdivided into smaller supporting units. Generalizations about length are not very helpful, since the paragraph should be an organic unit, shaped to fit the needs of the material. But it is worth considering that high school students tend to write fifty-word paragraphs while successful professionals average several hundred words. The writer who paragraphs like a newspaper editor—every two inches—throws away opportunities to signal the design of his composition to the reader. Two-inch divisions allow the writer to be careless and undisciplined, to dodge the requirements of emphasis and subordination, to string his thoughts along like a row of box houses in

Levittown. A paragraph need not be a skyscraper, but it should be a substantial construction with some parts highlighted, others subdued, and all of them controlled by a comprehensive plan.

Here is a characteristic paragraph from Henry Steele Commager's *The American Mind:*

> The American's attitude toward authority, rules, and regulations was the despair of bureaucrats and disciplinarians. Nowhere did he differ more sharply from his English cousins than in his attitude toward rules, for where the Englishman regarded the observance of a rule as a positive pleasure, to the American a rule was at once an affront and a challenge. His schools were almost without discipline, yet they were not on the whole disorderly, and the young girls and spinsters who taught them were rarely embarrassed. This absence of discipline in the schools reflected absence of discipline in the home. Parents were notoriously indulgent of their children and children notoriously disrespectful of parents, yet family life was on the whole happy, and most children grew up to be good parents and good citizens. The laxity of discipline in his armies was a scandal tolerated only because they somehow fought well and won battles. It seemed entirely natural that during the Civil War privates should elect their officers and that the greatest of the generals should so often see his plans miscarry because he hesitated to give firm orders to his subordinates or to insist upon obedience. If Lincoln did not pardon quite so many sleeping sentinels as folklore relates, it was characteristic that folklore should celebrate as a virtue a gesture so disruptive to all discipline.

Commager covers a lot of territory in this 224-word paragraph about American attitudes in the nineteenth century, but it is a well-organized, well-governed territory. He opens with a firm statement of his point—Americans had little respect for authority—and supports it with subordinate statements about American schools, home life, and military service. Each one of these subdivisions repeats the main point, using the same word ("his schools were almost without discipline"; "absence of discipline in the home"; "laxity of discipline in the armies"), and they relate so closely to one another that transition between them is easy, virtually inevitable: "This absence of discipline in the schools reflected absence of discipline in the home." Since armies are discussed last, Commager can move smoothly to his concluding symbol—the celebration of Lincoln's pardon of sleeping sentinels—which rounds out the idea established at the opening and contained in each of the eight sentences. So tight is the organization that the first five words, if joined to the last four, state the theme of the paragraph as a whole: "The American's attitude toward authority [was] disruptive to all discipline."

The structure of Commager's paragraph could be diagramed as follows:

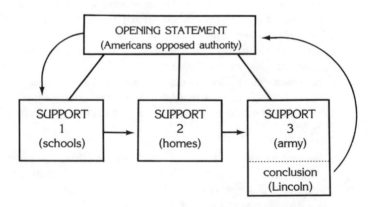

Simultaneously, another organizing principle is at work, that of contrast. We have:

Americans	against	bureaucrats
		disciplinarians
		English cousins

absence of discipline	against	authority
notoriously indulgent		rules
notoriously disrespectful		regulations
laxity		firm orders, obedience

rules as affronts and challenges	against	rules as pleasures

This contrast, like any competition or conflict, provides interest, and it also embodies the author's evaluation of the material he presents, an evaluation contained in yet another series of pairs:

schools were almost without discipline	yet	they were not on the whole disorderly
parents were notoriously indulgent...	yet	family life was on the whole happy
laxity of discipline in his armies...	[yet]	they somehow fought well and won battles

Hovering behind these explicit contrasts, and the language about battles and Englishmen, is an implicit reference to that other war in which American troops, undisciplined as they were, sent their "English cousins" packing. Professor Commager announces that he is no fool—he doesn't believe all the stories, the "folklore" about Lincoln—and he admits that authority has its claims, but like the nineteenth-century Americans he writes about, Commager celebrates as a virtue the American resistance to authority and regulations; he too thumbs a democratic nose at bureaucrats and disciplinarians.

A skeptic might suggest that Professor Commager's paragraph is too good, too well organized for the workaday world of ordinary communication. Such skepticism could be buttressed by current research, which suggests that many, even most, paragraphs do not have explicit thesis sentences. Few have such tight tripartite structure. Nevertheless, Commager's virtues of thesis control and organization are real, even though they may not always be so neatly incorporated into a single paragraph.

Parallelism is a trick of the expert writer whose phrases continue to echo in our cultural memory:

> Not that I loved Caesar less, but that I loved Rome more....As he was valiant, I honour him: but, as he was ambitious, I slew him.

> We shall fight in France, we shall fight on the seas and oceans, we shall fight with growing confidence and growing strength in the air, we shall defend our island, whatever the cost may be, we shall fight on the beaches, we shall fight on the landing grounds, we shall fight in the fields and in the streets, we shall fight in the hills; we shall never surrender.

> Shallow understanding from people of good will is more frustrating than absolute misunderstanding from people of ill will. Lukewarm acceptance is much more bewildering than outright rejection.

Even if your rhetoric does not have the thunder of Shakespeare, Churchill, or Martin Luther King, you should attempt to express coordinate ideas in coordinate forms. The simplest use of parallelism is to put equivalent units in a series into similar grammatical constructions: "The defendant was sentenced to a dishonorable discharge, that he had to forfeit all his pay and allowances, and in addition being required to serve six months' confinement at hard labor." This triple punishment would be easier on the reader if it were expressed as a series of prepositional objects: "to a dishonorable discharge, a forfeiture of all pay and allowances, and six months' confinement at hard labor." Infinitives would also do it: "to be dishonorably discharged, to forfeit all pay and allowances, and to be confined for six months at hard labor."

A more subtle lack of parallelism can be seen in the following sentence about Alabama in the 1840s. "As the advancing settlers pushed the backwoods farther back, roads overran footpaths, farmlands supplanted forests, and the council fires of the Creeks were replaced by weekly newspapers." The pattern here is new-old, new-old, old-new. The last clause should be reversed to take advantage of the formula that the reader recognizes in the first pair and expects in those that follow: "As the advancing settlers pushed the backwoods farther back, roads overran footpaths, farmlands supplanted forests, and weekly newspapers replaced the council fires of the Creeks."

There are many kinds of parallelisms, all of which involve repetition of one sort or another. Some use simple grammatical reiteration (to be discharged, to forfeit, to be confined). Others gain a rolling momentum through accumulation (in France, on the seas, in the air). Still others sharpen the expression on both ends with antithesis (Caesar less... Rome more). The trick is to keep some elements identical or similar and to vary others. George Bernard Shaw, in a satirical attack on high medical fees, demonstrates how parallels in

rhetoric can be used to shock the reader into seeing parallels in
content:

> That any sane nation, having observed that you could provide
> for the supply of bread by giving bakers a pecuniary interest in
> baking for you, should go on to give a surgeon a pecuniary
> interest in cutting off your leg, is enough to make one despair of
> political humanity.

Shaw manipulates his sentence to balance baking and surgery

> bakers...a pecuniary interest in baking for you
> surgeon...a pecuniary interest in cutting off your leg

and tightens the comparison by using the same phrase ("a
pecuniary interest") in the center of each.

Since parallelism often involves a series, it is interesting to
speculate on the effects produced by the number of items in
the series. According to Winston Weathers, an author "can
write the two-part series and create the aura of certainty and
confidence.... He can write the three-part series and create the
effect of the normal, the reasonable, the believable.... He can
write the four-or-more-part series and suggest the human,
emotional, diffuse, and inexplicable." Perhaps Weathers's
analysis helps to explain why we turn so often, almost
instinctively, to units of three for organizational structure as
well as rhetorical effect: *social, political,* and *economic; love,
honor,* and *obey; the world, the flesh,* and *the devil;* as easy as
ABC; "And for the support of this declaration ... we mutually
pledge to each other *our lives, our fortunes,* and *our sacred
honor*"; "government *of the people, by the people, for the
people,* shall not perish from the earth."

See **Connection.**

Precision.   "The difference between the almost right word and the right word is really a large matter," Mark Twain wrote in 1890, "'tis the difference between the lightning-bug and the lightning." One way to achieve precision, to eliminate the bugs, is to employ J. D. Salinger's technique of trying different words until an expression seems right. Another is to keep a dictionary close at hand and check the meanings of the words you plan to use, even those you think you are sure of. To return to simplistic virtues is not the same as to return to simple virtues. Uninterested-disinterested, egoist-egotist, prudent-prudish: these word pairs are not synonyms. A third way to achieve precision is to weigh carefully the connotations of words (what they suggest) as well as their denotations (explicit meanings). Political instruments are not the same as political tools. Connotations in one part of a sentence need to be lined up with the words in the rest of the sentence: "Everyone was there, from those of seventeen summers to those of seventy winters." And a writer must take care not to line up associations incongruously: "His reference to the sacred waters of the Ganges adds flavor to his writing." Connotation provides the fine adjustment that brings an idea into precise focus. It can also bring distortion, deliberate and perverse. *Time* magazine used to report that Harry Truman met with his cronies; President Eisenhower, however, consulted with his advisers.

See **Clichés, Jargon, Puffery, Slang, Weak intensifiers.**

Pronouns.   The lack of a clear pronoun reference constitutes a common problem, easily corrected. "Lionel beat his father, and his uncle laughed at him." To whom does the *him* refer, Lionel or father? For that matter, whose uncle, Lionel's or father's, does the laughing? This sort of ambiguity usually results from the inevitable fact that the writer is closer to his context than is his reader. The writer knows his characters— Lionel, father, uncle—and who is likely to be laughing at whom. The reader may be less certain and needs clear signposts, either in the precise distribution of the pronouns or in the meaning of the text itself. If the sentence above were the third example of Lionel being ridiculed by his uncle, there would be no problem. Remember that, other things being equal, a pronoun refers back to the nearest preceding logical noun.

A less contextual and more grammatical problem—one designed to harass schoolmarms and sell red pencils—is the lack of agreement between pronoun and antecedent. "It is every citizen's duty to interest themselves in conservation" strikes most educated Americans as a blunder. (The British are more liberal in these matters.) "Each person drank their tea" appears to be either ungrammatical or unsanitary. But this use of *their,* ungrammatical or not, has long filled the gap in English resulting from the lack of a singular possessive pronoun that refers to both sexes. "David and his date drank his and her tea" is awkward and possibly confusing (both sip each others' tea?), as is the presumably correct "Neither David nor his date drank his tea" (what about her tea?). In an era of raised consciousness, the singular *their* will undoubtedly flourish unless we come up with a singular bisexual pronoun. My candidate is *hir,* a word that combines the sounds of *his* and *her,* and one which could pass for a shortened form of *their.*

Anyone, each, either, everybody, everyone, no one, and *someone* take singular verbs; *all* and *none* can go either way. Collective nouns such as *class, committee, faculty, jury, majority, orchestra,* and *public* are singular if they represent a collection conceived as one unit *(the faculty is part of university governance),* plural if they represent a collection of individuals *(the faculty are finally ready to vote).* The indefinite pronouns *(anyone, each, everyone,* and the like) usually require singular possessive pronouns *(everyone pledged his support),* but may take plural forms if the sense demands *(everyone scattered, looking for their clothes).*

Proofreading. Careless mistakes, even small ones, distract the most sympathetic reader; they give an obstinate reader an opportunity to devote his attention to trivia. Spelling, for example, seems to be a superstition in our society. Editors, employers, reviewing judges, and professors all seem to assume that if you can't spell correctly you probably aren't able to think accurately—an assumption analogous to the notion that a man who trips getting out of airplanes can somehow not be trusted to govern a nation. But even for the non-superstitious, reading an essay full of spelling errors is like driving a car on railroad tracks. And often mistakes can derail your meaning completely: "Odysseus felt secretly compelled to flea his own house." If you write "a grizzly picture," meaning "grisly," your reader drops the line of thought momentarily to look for the bears. If you write seeking employment in a letter addressed to the "University of Vaginia," by the time your reader finishes showing the letter to his colleagues and indulging himself in hypothetical replies, it is difficult for him to take your qualifications very seriously.

Proofreading is a key act, the last step in the process of writing. Two readings are required. The first consists of a rapid survey for meaning, coherence, connections. The second, a check on details of correctness, differs from a normal reading. You must consciously slow down your eye scan to focus on every individual letter and mark of punctuation. Good proofreaders often develop habits to deliberately break up the usual process of reading for meaning. Some use rulers or pencils or fingers to direct attention; others proofread from back to front. The psycho-linguistic principle behind these habits, according to Frank Smith, is that the brain "identifies letters, words, [and] meaning, but not at the same time; that is, the brain can perform these three distinct tasks on the same visual information, but it can only do one task at a time."

See **Spelling**.

Puffery. *Beautiful, enchanting, exciting, fabulous, fantastic, incredible, marvelous, thrilling, tremendous, wonderful.* Give these words back to their natural parents—the writers of advertisements for soap, election campaigns, Disney World, and Oldsmobiles.

But this exhortation, like most others in the field of writing, can sometimes be successfully ignored. As Amy Lowell put it, "any theory carried too far ends in sterility." Richard Kain hit upon the perfect title, *Fabulous Voyager,* for his book about James Joyce's *Ulysses.* Somehow "fabulous" seems not too strong for the Greek hero's adventures with Calypso, Cyclops, and Circe; or the modern protagonist's journey through Dublin in 1904. And Kain takes advantage of the word's root meaning—of the nature of a fable. The reader discovers that "fabulous voyager," like a palimpsest, contains layered meanings that apply to Odysseus, to Leopold Bloom, and finally to all mankind. The point is that appropriate opportunities for using these words do exist, but they are rare.

Punctuation is often responsible for a variety of errors that cause composition teachers to bristle in the margins: "comma splice," "fragment," "awkward," "logic," "restrictive."

Take the **comma splice**: "Mrs. Walker's statements came within the exception to the hearsay rule relating to declarations against interest, that exception has been restated by the Supreme Court in *Breedon v. Independent Fire Ins. Co.*" The problem is simply that two discrete sentences are fused with a comma, rather than being separated with a period. If the meanings of two sentences are very close, a semicolon can be used. If a second sentence continues the first—explains or interprets or qualifies it—a dash or a colon is appropriate.

While the comma splice creates a double sentence, the **fragment**, which usually omits either the subject or the verb, or is a dependent clause standing alone, makes only half a sentence: "Not for the present"; "A question of murder"; "Which was the ultimate result of the report." Common in speech, frequent in casual writing, possible but rare in formal prose, the fragment must be used with discernment. The rule seems to be that if you can't recognize a fragment, you shouldn't use one. If you know the difference, then it is permissible. This paradoxical principle applies to many exceptions to the rules of writing, as well as to breaking other kinds of rules. It is possible to steal second base, but only if you know what you are doing. And run fast.

Perhaps the most common punctuation error in mature writing is the **uncompleted comma pair**. The writer starts to set off part of a sentence with two commas, but inserts only one: "It is alleged that the realtor, through fraud and misrepresentation induced the plaintiffs to sell their home for less than the market price." The answer is either to complete the pair (here by adding a comma after "misrepresentation") if the phrase in question could be omitted without altering the meaning, or to leave out both commas if the phrase is necessary to the meaning of the sentence. (The comma after realtor should be omitted if fraud is an essential part of the allegation.) Thus a comma or two can radically affect the sense of a statement. "Lawyers who drink often make incoherent arguments" is a reasonable proposition about the debilitating effects of alcohol on members of the bar. The addition of commas—"Lawyers, who drink, often make incoherent arguments"—creates a dramatic change: lawyers as a class become by definition both alcoholic and incoherent.

Commas, then, often come in pairs. So do dashes—which highlight the enclosed material—and parentheses (which tend to subordinate it).

A few reminders:

The **apostrophe** is used to indicate omission (*don't* for *do not*), possession (the *king's* crown), and plurals of letters and numbers (mind your *p's* and *q's* or you'll be at *6's* and *7's*). The use of the apostrophe for both omission and possession creates understandable confusion with *it's*, where the apostrophe is employed in its role as a signal of omission (*it's* = it is) and not as a signal of possession. None of the possessive pronouns—*his, hers, yours, ours, theirs,* or *its*—takes an apostrophe.

The singular possessive is formed by adding the apostrophe followed by *s*; the plural possessive by adding just the apostrophe (assuming that the plural ends in *s*; if it does not, add apostrophe *s*, as in women's rights):

H. N. Smith	Smith's book
the Smiths	the Smiths' house

These rules are supposed to hold even for nouns ending in *s*:

H. M. Jones	Jones's history
the Joneses	the Joneses' vacation

But exceptions in the singular created by the difficulty of pronouncing several *s* sounds together, especially in words of more than one syllable, are common:

Thucydides' exile

Jesus' sayings

Czolgosz' execution

Certain possessive forms, though technically correct, can become cumbersome. It is good policy to be careful with inanimate possessives (discussion at the *New York Times* dinner, not discussion at the *New York Times's* dinner) and with multiple possessives (an announcement by Merrill Lynch, Pierce, Fenner and Smith; not Merrill Lynch, Pierce, Fenner and Smith's announcement).

The **colon** is a mark of introduction used before an example, a series, or a second independent clause that continues or explains the first: "In a democracy there can be but one fundamental test of citizenship: are you using such gifts as you possess for or against the people."

Experienced writers avoid the slingshot effect created by dropping in a colon after the verb: "The three passions that have governed my life are: love, knowledge, and pity." The sentence that Bertrand Russell actually wrote illustrates the skillful use of the colon: "Three passions, simple but overwhelmingly strong, have governed my life: the longing for love, the search for knowledge, and unbearable pity for the suffering of mankind."

Scholars often use two **commas** in a series of three items (red, white, and blue), journalists one (red, white and blue). The scholar would argue that A, B, and C indicate three separate items (A B C) whereas A, B and C could mean only two (A BC): "The statutes concerning environmental protection, public health, and safety were passed by the legislature." That statement refers to three statutes. Omitting the comma after health leaves the number of statutes in doubt. The second comma in a series of three becomes more important as the series becomes longer and more complex:

A few days before the transfer, the Bernadinis deposited into this account a check for $233.72 payable to Mrs. Bernadini for wages, a check for $386.00 for Workman's Compensation

benefits payable to Mr. Bernardini and others for $1,780.36
payable to them jointly for Social Security disability benefits.

Here the author could keep his reader afloat by tossing him a
comma after "payable to Mr. Bernardini."

The **dash** is made in typing with two hyphens and no spaces
on either side. It is used—often overused—to separate
parenthetical elements in a sentence and to join closely
connected parts: "Every woman should marry—and no man"
(Disraeli).

The **exclamation point** usually creates a corny or melo-
dramatic effect in serious prose, and its use to point up
discrepancy or irony is nearly always a cheap shot: "The
welfare applicant said she has not had any clothes for a year
and has been visited regularly by the clergy!" If you make a
joke don't spoil it by nudging the reader in the ribs.

The **hyphen** signals a connection, although one would never
know it from packing cases. A case of Budweiser, according to
the label, contains "4-6 packs, 24-12 oz. bottles," which
presumably means 4 6-packs, 24 12-oz. bottles. Beer cartons
aside, the hyphen is used to divide words at the end of a line
and to create compound adjectives preceding nouns: *nineteenth-century* decision; *sloe-eyed* houri. By convention, if the
first word in a compound modifier ends in *ly*, the hyphen is
omitted: a *carefully worded* request.

Some compound words, halfway along in the process of
unification, are spelled with a hyphen. Shakespeare used
"halfe way to her heart" (1596); Matthew Prior said "her
bodice half-way she unlaced" (1696); Goldsmith referred to
"halfway home" (1766). A current dictionary will indicate
what stage any particular compound has reached. Most words
prefixed by *self* (*self-conscious, self-educated*) and *well* (*well-
known, well-worded*) take the hyphen. Those prefixed with
semi (*semiaquatic*) and *over* (*overbearing*) usually do not.

The **parenthesis** (Greek, "to put in beside") is used to insert explanatory or qualifying information of less importance than the main text, although the information should be brief and not interrupt the reader. Often a parenthesis signals the point where a sentence went awry:

> Although in neither instance did the city pass an ordinance requiring the clerk to pay collected fees to the treasurer (which the Court thinks is necessary, so as to put the clerk on notice that paying collected fees to the treasurer is his legal duty), the two cases may be distinguished.

It would be best to recast this sentence, writing in the parenthetical information and taking out the parenthesis.

Quotation marks around questionable or slangy words and phrases (the "smart money"; a serious "goof"; she went "all the way") usually indicate the author's suspicion about the suitability of the expression. Don't apologize for a doubtful expression with quotation marks; avoid it entirely, using instead diction that is appropriate to both your purpose and your audience.

The **semicolon** can be thought of as a large comma that provides more of a stop than a regular comma, less than a period. It is used to link closely related independent clauses:

> I don't get any older; my students just keep getting younger.

and to separate units of a sentence that have commas inside them:

> In determining the weight given to testimony the jury may consider the demeanor of the witnesses on the stand; their manner of testifying; their temper, feeling, or bias, if any has been shown; and their opportunity for knowing the truth.

Quotations.   Long quotations of prose (over fifty words) and
three lines or more of poetry are normally set off from the rest
of the text, are single-spaced, and do not require quotation
marks (unless there are quotation marks in the original) since
single-spacing indicates quotation. Single-spaced prose quotations should be indented ten spaces; poetry is centered.

   To indicate an omission within a quotation use an ellipsis—
three or four periods separated in typing by spacing (. . . not
. . .). Use the three-period ellipsis for omissions within a
sentence. Use the four-period ellipsis when the omitted matter
immediately precedes the period ending a sentence. (Thus the
additional period is the period at the end of the quoted
sentence.)

   Take the following sentence from Paul Fussell:

> There seems to be one dominating form of modern
> understanding; it is essentially ironic; and it originates largely in
> the application of mind and memory to the events of the Great
> War.

The three-period ellipsis indicates internal omission:

> There seems to be one dominating form of modern
> understanding . . . and it originates largely in the application of
> mind and memory to the events of the Great War.

The four-period ellipsis includes the terminal sentence period:

> There seems to be one dominating form of modern
> understanding; it is essentially ironic . . . .

   It is usually unnecessary to begin a quotation with an
ellipsis or to surround an obviously incomplete quotation with
a fence of periods: Daniel Webster maintains that the law

" . . . has honoured us, may we honour it . . . ." Keep the reader's momentum intact by nestling a quoted fragment in the arms of the surrounding sentence: Daniel Webster maintains that the law "has honoured us, may we honour it." Since a well-placed ellipsis connects parts of a quotation smoothly and grammatically (and, of course, without distortion of the original meaning), there should be no need for punctuation preceding the ellipsis (, . . .).

Periods and commas fall inside final quotation marks; colons and semicolons fall outside. This complicated custom is said to date back to Renaissance typographers who apparently thought that it pleased the eye more to have short punctuation tucked inside quotation marks, tall punctuation outside. This convention cannot be defended logically, but—like the convention of right-hand traffic in America—it is helpful to have everyone following the same rules. (The British now put periods outside final quotation marks, but then they also drive on the left side of the road.)

Question marks and exclamation points (and here there is logic) are placed inside or outside final quotation marks, depending on whether the questions and exclamations go with the quoted matter or with the sentence as a whole.

Use square brackets to insert material within a quotation that is not part of the quotation: "The Kitlik [a river in the western end of the Brooks Range, in Alaska, where John McPhee was camped] has formed with the Salmon River a raised, flat sand-and-gravel mesopotamia—a good enough campsite, and, as a glance can tell, a fishing site to exaggerate the requirements of dinner."

Introduce quotations smoothly into your prose, the way an experienced diver enters the water:

Henry James maintains that when the writer does his work well, "then the reader does quite half the labor."

Avoid the splashy cannonball:

> Henry James in his essay makes the following statement which is here excerpted in part: "When he [i.e., the writer] makes him [the reader] ill, that is, makes him indifferent, he does no work; the writer does all. When he makes him well, that is, makes him interested, then the reader does quite half the labor."

Quotations must be scrupulously accurate, but one change is allowed. If you are incorporating into your sentence a quoted passage that begins with a capital, you may change it to a lower-case letter. If you are beginning a sentence with a quoted word that is not capitalized in the original, change the first letter to a capital.

Finally, use no more of a quotation than is necessary. The writer who quotes twenty sentences often has to italicize or underline the two key ones, and then add a pompous note: "emphasis supplied." Throw away the note, the emphasis, and the eighteen unnecessary sentences.

Revision. The student who boasts of one-draft papers should be reminded of Ben Jonson's reply to the players who boasted that Shakespeare never blotted out a line: "Would he had blotted a thousand." Jonson may or may not have been right, but without Shakespeare's genius, you had best be prepared to revise. Revision serves many purposes, but the most important is breaking out of the self-indulgent solipsism of early drafts—where you understand what you are trying to say—and making certain that your reader understands also. Revision is the point at which you bring your work out of your study and into the world. It is the time to remind yourself that your reader does not share your angle of vision, your bias, your recent familiarity with the subject, your ability to read into your prose what you did not write, your fond maternal patience with the waywardness of your own creation. It is the moment when you steel yourself for sacrifice, for throwing things away. The writer who cannot bear to part with phrases and sentences, no matter how deformed, probably preserves his extracted teeth in a jar and saves his toenail clippings.

On one hand, revision requires that some points too easily assumed by the writer must be made more elaborate and more explicit for the reader (see **Ambiguity**). On the other hand, revision also provides an opportunity to trim down points that are belabored by the writer in early drafts (see **Obvious statements**). For the last step in the process, see **Proofreading**.

Sexist language and non-sexist language both create problems, as do both sex and non-sex. Moderate indulgence is perhaps the best advice. A strategic use of *he or she*, *his or her* may help win over readers offended by the cavalier assumption that the masculine pronoun includes the fifty-one per cent of the users of the English language who happen not to be male. But don't overdo it. Changing all your *he*'s to *he or she* will cripple your expression. The Woonsocket Rhode Island City Council recently made a sensible alteration in the city personnel ordinance when they changed *utility men* to *utility persons*. But when the Council went on to turn *manholes* into *personholes*, they put Woonsocket on the map—right on the coast of absurdity.

Sensitive writers would do well to avoid the many expressions in our language that imply female inferiority. Somehow we say *weak sisters*, but never *weak brothers*. Co-ed, denying its *co*, refers only to women. We use one term of address—*Mr.*—for men, two—*Miss* and *Mrs.*—for women, thus implying that marital status is more important, more definitive, for females than for males. The new coinage *Ms.* (plural *Mses.* or *Mss.*) seems to be sticking, probably because it argues for equal linguistic rights and avoids awkward moments in business correspondence. As for *Chairman, Chairperson, Madame Chairman*, or *Chair* to refer to a person in authority, choose the term that seems most appropriate for the particular audience. *Chairman* and similar words are simultaneously masculine and neuter. No one can ignore the connotations of masculinity sprung loose by chair*man*, yet *man* has also meant "person" in English for over a thousand years. *Woman* itself, originally *wifmann*, "female person," illustrates the ambiguity of gender ineradicably built into the language. Those women who object to the presence of a man in their word can take some historical comfort from the fact that *mann* in Old English generally meant "a human being irrespective of sex or age" *(OED)*, while the words used to designate feminine and masculine—*wif* and *wer*—have survived in *wife* and *werewolf*.

See **Pronouns.**

Slang words and expressions are ingenious new coinages or new uses of established words: "Me and this dude saw smokey so we hit our wheels and split." Many slang expressions inspire admiration and condemnation simultaneously. H. L. Mencken notes that slang is striking, pungent, picturesque, energetic, metaphorical, defiant, exuberant—"the most powerful of all the stimulants that keep the language alive and growing." Yet, in the same discussion, Mencken suggests that most slang is "bilge," especially "the numerous catch phrases that have little if any precise meaning but simply delight the moron by letting him show that he knows the latest."

Like the ephemeral May fly, slang expressions usually have their day and die. Nothing seems deader than yesterday's slang: *chick, masher, lounge lizard, nifty, jazzy, red-hot mamma, schmoo, moola, square shooter, the real McCoy, hip, hubba-hubba, groovy*. But occasionally a phrase sticks permanently, and one wonders if any of these current slang expressions will be in use in the twenty-first century:

A-O.K.	hang-up	rap
Afro	junk food	rip off
blast off	laid back (See *cool*)	split
bread (for cash)	macho	threads (for clothes)
bug (annoy; eavesdrop)	nerd (an uncool dude)	up tight
busted (without bread; arrested)	off the wall	where I'm at (the stage that apparently follows "where I'm coming from")
cool (suave, un-emotional, O.K.)	porno	
cop out	relate to ("he can't relate to his employer," or better, "he can't relate to his father")	workaholic
counterculture		x-rated
hacking it		

Such expressions are usually avoided in careful writing, but not always. It is a question of skillful application. A current phrase, repeated several times by Richard Nixon in the Frost interviews, is "the bottom line"—meaning conclusion, result, total cost, what it all adds up to. To say "the bottom line was that I quit my summer job" sounds ludicrous. But an essay that quoted the ex-president's use of the phrase might turn it to an effective conclusion: "For Richard Nixon, the bottom line was resignation."

The same is true of clichés and jargon. If you can put a new spin on an old expression, you can turn a dull phrase into an interesting one. "Necessity," according to Mark Twain, "is the mother of taking chances." After losing to Eisenhower, Adlai Stevenson noted that "to the victor belong the toils." Pogo trained Captain Perry's guns in a new direction: "We have met the enemy, and they are us." If you are using quotations and literary allusions, remember that good usage is not guaranteed by the power or beauty of the original expression. It must be both fresh and appropriate in its new context. A postmaster who swears in a clerk by telling him to "ask not what your country can do for you, ask what you can do for your country" will probably not hasten delivery of the mail.

The writer who strives for the colloquial ease of speech without descending to slang will also wish to avoid excessive informality: "Agnew had no class"; "Odysseus and a couple of guys had a tremendous blast with Circe." Close relatives, also to be avoided, are corny remarks ("George Eliot alias Mary Ann Evans"), melodrama ("Booker T. Washington, prophetically born in Franklin County, became the first black man to follow Benjamin Franklin's model for success"), smirking understatement ("her parents were slightly upset when she demolished the car"), unwarranted overstatement ("I made a fatal mistake on that fateful evening"; "he was half dead with embarrassment"). Understatement and overstatement, since they provide contrast, are indispensable weapons of the humorist. But like most weapons, they are safe only in experienced hands.

See **Clichés, Jargon,** and **Neologism.**

Specific details are often more vivid, accurate, and persuasive than general statements. If you describe a sonnet as simple, beautiful, and effective, and let it go at that, your reader can say, so is a shark. An essay that cannot distinguish between a poem and a fish is in trouble. State the real point, not a bland summary of it. "The popular press criticized the immigrants; even those who did not condemn them limited their sympathies to charity" takes on more bite when the same points are detailed: "The popular press claimed that America was becoming 'a dumping ground for Europe's rubbish.' Those who did not condemn the immigrants sent them old clothes wrapped in newspapers." A generalizing writer, in the Pentagon perhaps, might say "For a long time the Navy has had to deal with the problems of overindulgence, inter-personal relations, and corporal punishment." Winston Churchill put it more sharply to Parliament: "I'll give you the traditions of the Royal Navy—rum, buggery, and the lash." Don't say "he published in major American magazines" but "he published in *The New Yorker* and *Harper's* (or the *Huntington Library Quarterly* and the *Renaissance Quarterly;* or the *Reader's Digest* and *TV Guide*). Such details are not only more striking, but more informative; "major" can mean a number of things. Instead of saying "he reacted to the situation," state what the reaction was: "he swerved off the road." "They had an interesting relationship" is not as meaningful as "they were in love." "There will be important implications in the Near East" doesn't state the point: "the price of oil will be raised." Words like *reaction, situation, interesting, relationship,* and *implication* offer the shell of the lobster without the meat.

The writer usually comes to generalizations inductively, down the path of detail. Leading the reader down that same path is more likely to persuade than simply springing a conclusion on him. At the same time, the writer may well want to begin with a generalization so that the reader will know the target for the specifics in advance. Thus good writing is often simultaneously deductive and inductive—opening with a general proposition and then developing details that lead to a conclusion in harmony with the original proposition. Most skilled writers develop a rhythm of interrelated generalizations and specifics. Specificity is stressed in this entry not because it is the only virtue, but because it is one commonly neglected by beginning and intermediate writers.

Speech and writing have a lovers' quarrel. On one hand, as E. D. Hirsch puts it, "writing must secure meaning by special techniques which are not normally required in oral speech"— techniques that make up for the lack of a specific personal context, gesture, and oral intonation and stress. On the other hand, experienced writing instructors have for years urged students with wordlogged compositions to read their writing aloud in order to hear what is wrong. These notions are opposite but not contradictory. Written prose must separate itself from the spoken word to convey meaning effectively, but it should not get too far away or it will be static and artificial. The trick is to keep the advantages of speech (rhythm, ease, idiomatic phrasing) and to shed the disadvantages (meandering structure, imprecision, slangy phrasing).

Some writers, breezy to a fault in conversation, stiffen when faced with a formal paper and write *societal* for *social* or *trebled* for *tripled* just to show the reader they mean business. Serious prose does not mean prose that is pretentious, or rigid, or unnecessarily embellished. Aim for a comfortable middle ground, somewhere between blue jeans and a tuxedo.

See **Ambiguity.**

Spelling. The complexities of English orthography stem from two historical circumstances. The first is that English has many ancestors. Germanic in origin, English acquired much of its vocabulary from Latin as well as from French and other Latin-based Romance languages. And English (especially American English) has shown a democratic openness to words from Hindustani, Chinese, Hebrew, Russian, Arabic, Malay; as well as to the languages of West Africans, Polynesians,

American Indians, and many others. A second complication was created by the invention of printing in the mid-fifteenth century, which fixed spelling while pronunciation continued to evolve. As a result there are about three hundred ways to spell the forty sounds used in English. No wonder G. B. Shaw could suggest "ghoti" as a possible spelling of fish (gh as in rou*gh*; o as in w*o*men; ti as in na*ti*on).

Mere rules cannot create order from this apparent chaos, but two are worth remembering. The old "i before e except after c" rhyme (when "ie" is pronounced *ee*) solves many problems, but the exceptions to the rule constitute an important subset: neither financier seized either species [of] weird leisure. A second useful rule organizes the seemingly erratic behavior of final consonants confronted with suffixes: Double the final consonant before a suffix if the accent is on the final syllable, the final consonant is single, it is preceded by a single vowel, and the suffix begins with a vowel. Thus, *sinned, occurred, submitted*; but *benefited, appealed, shipment*. Sometimes greater attention to pronunciation can help. People who say "diptheria," "disasterous," "Febuary," "geneology," "mathmatics," and "sophmore" often begin to spell that way.

The following twenty words are among those most commonly misspelled in English:

absence	definite	occur
accommodate	dependent	omit
all right	despair	privilege
apparent	existence	separate
argument	lonely	supersede
commitment	noticeable	truly
criticize	occasion	

British spellings *(connexion, defence, foetus, grey, judgement, labour, practise)* have an exotic charm that should be resisted.

For the incorrigible there are spelling books that contain about a hundred undefined words to the page, thus making it possible to check spelling at three times the speed of thumbing through a conventional dictionary. See Houghton Mifflin's *The Word Book* and G. & C. Merriam's *Instant Word Guide.*

Thesis.   According to Poe in his review of Hawthorne's *Twice-Told Tales*, an author begins by conceiving "a certain single effect to be wrought.... If his very first sentence tend not to the out-bringing of this effect, then in his very first step has he committed a blunder. In the whole composition there should be no word written of which the tendency, direct or indirect, is not to the one pre-established design." Poe overstates the case, but his point is important. A careful pre-established design or thesis is often the difference between a generalized discussion and an essay that achieves the writer's intention with precision and finality. Thinking about a subject may well begin with a loosely defined area (women in nineteenth-century American fiction) but that area must be narrowed to a topic (ambiguous portraits of women in the Gilded Age political novel) and finally sharpened to a thesis (the political novels of Henry James, Henry Adams, and J. W. DeForest postulate simultaneously women's fireside superiority and their worldly inferiority by creating fictional women who are ineffective political advisers, corrupt lobbyists, and irrelevant reformers).

Conceiving the thesis is the crucial last step in the process of thought that must precede serious writing. A solid thesis enables one to decide what comes first and what second, which details should be kept and which eliminated. It is, for both writer and reader, the thread through the labyrinth of research.

Once you have a thesis—one that explains the data as you see it, one you can believe in—your next task is normally that of argumentation.* You wish to persuade your reader to your point of view, convince him or her that your conclusions are the ones that best explain your evidence. Two things should be kept in mind as you conduct a civilized argument on paper, both designed to prevent your reader from accusing you of reducing complexity or concealing contrary evidence. Present some of your material in a preliminary raw form; then your reader can watch as you perform your act of intelligent interpretation and be carried along in the process. And plan a structure that takes possible objections into account, that allows for some of the difficult cargo that doesn't quite fit—without, of course, overturning your boat. Assuming your point is A, here are six different possibilities for organizing a paper:

1. A
    Not B
    A

2. Appears to be B
    but is really A

3. A is the truth
    A^1 not B^1
    A^2 not B^2
    A^3 not B^3
    hence A

---

*This discusssion deliberately ignores the traditional rhetorical categories of exposition, description, narration, and argumentation. These terms are pedagogical rather than descriptive. That is, they are used to explain rhetorical modes to beginning students and to design exercises: "Write a paragraph that explains an idea; then write a paragraph that describes a person." Real paragraphs, however, are almost always mixed. They employ exposition, description, and narration together and they almost always seek to persuade.

4. Some truth in B
    but more in A

5. Of the various possibilities—A, B, C, D, and E—A best
    explains the evidence.

6. A, B, C, D, and E are all true, and all are generally related
    to the topic. But given my thesis, A needs the most
    discussion. Thus I will focus on A and subordinate the
    others: b c A d e.

See **Coherence.**

Titles.   Since writing communicates by presenting patterns that
allow the reader to make a series of successful predictions, the
logical place to begin such patterns is at the beginning—with
the title. A good title announces the meal to come and whets
the reader's appetite as well: *The Machine in the Garden, Civil
Disobedience, Bury My Heart at Wounded Knee, The Lonely
Crowd.* Titles such as "Critical Analysis," "The Plays of
Shakespeare," and "A Slice of American History" should be
packaged and sold to insomniacs.

Titles of books, pamphlets, periodicals, newspapers, plays,
films, symphonies, and operas are italicized in print and
underlined in typing; as are works—poems, essays, lectures,
and reports—that appear as separate publications. Quotation
marks are used with chapter titles, articles in periodicals, and
essays and poems published as part of a collection. The
distinction is analogous to the nautical differentiation between
a boat and a ship—a boat is a smaller craft, capable of being
hoisted aboard a ship. Use underlining, then, for the larger
literary work, quotation marks for the smaller.

See **Footnote and bibliographic forms**.

Typing conventions.   Skip one space after a **comma**, a **colon**, or
a **semicolon**; two spaces after a **period** ending a sentence.

A **dash** is made with two hypens--without spacing.

Double-space lines throughout any normal paper, with the exception of long quotations, footnotes, and bibliography. If copy is being prepared for a printer, double-space everything.

Initials of persons should be spaced: W. E. B. Du Bois. Other initials are normally not spaced: Washington, D.C.; M.A.; P.M. Many well-known abbreviations, especially those that are acronyms, drop the period and are never spaced: WPA, ROTC, DNA, GNP; VISTA, CORE, CARE.

Italic type, indicated by underlining, is used for titles (see **Titles**) and for foreign words and phrases (with the exception of those—like laissez-faire—that have become naturalized English citizens).

Margins should be generous (1 to 1½ inches) on all sides. Indent the beginning of a paragraph five spaces from the left margin. Indent long, single-spaced quotations ten spaces from the left margin.

Final **quotation marks** go outside periods and commas, inside colons and semicolons.

Word division at the end of a line should conform to syllabication, which any dictionary will indicate. Avoid leaving single letters stranded (dictionar-y) or creating bizarre double effects with partial words ("There are several cases of impeti-go in the hospital"). A ragged right-hand margin is often preferable to broken words, especially when sending copy to a printer, since he may confuse words spelled with a hyphen with those divided by a hyphen.

See **Punctuation, Quotations, Titles.**

Usage: some particular cases. Usage changes, and the writer must be careful to aim for the safe middle ground between truculent conservatives, who insist that what was good enough for King James is good enough for them, and giddy butterflies of fashion, who flit from one brief linguistic bloom to another. It is silly to insist on a distinction between *people* and *persons* ("five persons were there"), when most people—or persons— no longer recognize it. It is equally silly to litter serious prose with passing colloquialisms: "Henry James finally gets it all together in *The Portrait of a Lady*"; "Justice Cardozo's opinion opened a real can of worms."

Part of the fun of language is watching words change: *the keper of the bokes* became a *book keeper*, then a *book-keeper*, and finally a streamlined one-word *bookkeeper*. *Mad money* originally meant cash carried by a girl to pay her way home in case she quarreled with her date. Now it means a supply of extra money set aside for impulsive, reckless expenditure—a turn made possible by two colloquial meanings of *mad*— angry and crazy.

These changes occur more rapidly in speech than in writing. It took centuries for the *keper of the bokes* to become a *bookkeeper*, but pronunciation alters in decades. A word in transition at the moment is *harass*. Dictionaries and newscasters have long insisted on the pronunciation *har'əs*, but even they are changing to *hə ras.'* The accent is shifting to the rear, as if the etymology were to harry one's ass rather than the Old French *harer*, to set a dog on. Usage now seems so evenly divided that there is virtually no middle ground—*har'əs* gives one an air of pedantry, *hə ras'* the nudge of vulgarity. Time will solve the problem, for our children will say *hə ras'* without a qualm.

Many of the so-called rules of language are simply uses rigidified over the years. The neighborhood bridge club would undoubtedly ridicule the person who voiced the *h* in herbs, but they would be just as hard on someone who said " 'erbicide," or " 'erbivorous." Logic is not much help here. All you can do is learn the rules, not for their own sake, but to give you the choice of following suit, if a given usage serves your intellectual and social needs; or not, if it don't. Splitting an infinitive and ending a sentence with a preposition are not sins against good usage, but people who think they are represent an audience up with which you may have to put.

Common problems of usage for intermediate writers include the following:

aggravate/irritate   In formal use *aggravate* (from the Latin *aggravare*, to make heavier) means "to make worse," not "to irritate."

a historian/an historian   The indefinite article *a* is used before consonants: *an* is used before vowels and silent *h* *(hour)*. Since the *h* in *history, hotel*, and *harbinger* is now pronounced, these and similar words should be preceded by *a*, not *an*.

between/among   Use *between* (Old English "by two") with two objects normally, *among* (Old English "in a crowd") with three or more.

compare to/compare with   These expressions are differentiated by writers who pride themselves on fine distinctions. *Compare to* is used for general similarity and metaphor: "Shall I compare thee to a summer's day?" *Compare with* suggests a close examination in order to detect both similarities and differences: "SALT II negotiators compared Russia's ballistic missile system with that of the United States."

data is/data are   *Data* is the Latin plural of *datum*, but millions of users construe it as singular, so we may as well sail with the tide. A singular verb—"The data *is* correct"—seems perfectly acceptable. In a few decades, data will probably join other Latin plurals like *agenda*, whose singularity in English goes unquestioned.

deprecate/depreciate   *Deprecate* (Latin "pray against") in strict use means "to disapprove." In common parlance, however, especially in the expression *self-deprecate*, it has come to mean "depreciate" or "belittle," perhaps because depreciate seems to be increasingly reserved for financial matters.

due to   According to traditionalists *due to* means "caused by," not "because of": his divorce was due to dipsomania; she divorced him because of [not due to] his drunkenness. If this mildly useful but often ignored rule is followed, then a sentence cannot begin with *due to*. The lumbering phrase *due to the fact that* should always be avoided.

either/or   Avoid *either/or* and *and/or* in formal writing. These combinations are often unclear and they usually impede the reader.

ending with a preposition   The rule in English against ending a sentence with a preposition was based erroneously on Latin grammar, and can safely be ignored. A preposition is a perfectly good word to end a sentence with.

etc.   Use of this abbreviation for the Latin *et cetera*, "and others," often confesses that you really can't think of anything else, but you hope the reader will fill in the blank for himself.

farther/further   *Farther* comes from the Middle English *ferther*, which is simply a variant of *further*. Traditionally this slight difference has been employed to indicate a difference in meaning—*farther* for physical distance ("farther from the town"), *further* for figurative uses ("we talked further"). A good deal of crossing over occurs in usage, especially when the meaning of a statement is figurative but still calls up the idea of physical distance: "I will discuss that point further on"; "I will discuss that point farther on." *Further* is probably the better choice in such cases.

fewer/less Careful writers use *fewer* for countable quantity (fewer heroes), *less* for collective quantity (less courage)—a distinction Safeway is undermining ("Rapid checkout lane, eight items or less"), but one to be adhered to in writing.

hanged/hung *Hanged* is the traditional past participle for stringing up people, *hung* for stringing up clothes, pictures, mistletoe.

hopefully Some usage experts insist, shrilling against the wind, that *hopefully* should be limited to its literal meaning, "full of hope," and should not be used to mean "I hope" or "let us hope."

I am not so careful as/I am not as careful as *So* was long preferred with negative statements.

I feel bad/I feel badly The interestingly named copulative verbs—*feel, taste, smell, sound, be, become, appear, remain, seem, look*—are traditionally followed by adjectives rather than adverbs since they link the noun subject of a sentence to a noun modifier: "it appears solid"; "the peach tasted sweet." Conversely, verbs that do not join subject to description are normally modified by adverbs rather than adjectives: "it rings solidly"; "she sang sweetly." Thus "I feel bad" refers to the speaker's condition (I feel bad); "I feel badly" refers to his ability to feel (I feel badly).

if I were he/if I was he The subjunctive mood (if I *were* he) continues to disappear in informal English, perhaps because the *if* has replaced the verb tense as the main signal of an unlikely condition or one contrary to fact.

imply/infer *Imply* means to suggest; *infer* means to deduce. The speaker implies; the listener infers.

interpretative/interpretive The shortened form is coming into standard usage, probably by way of streamlined pronunciation.

it is I/it is me   *It is me* is gaining ground in this battle of the cases, especially when the statement is contracted: *it's me.* Undoubtedly the preponderance of subject-verb-object constructions in English works against the formal rule, honored in writing, which calls for the nominative case after the verb *to be.*

lie/lay   The increasing tide of confusion between the intransitive verb *lie* (to rest: lie, lay, lain) and the transitive verb *lay* (to place: lay, laid, laid) rolls on in spite of rules, textbooks, and careful users. The most common problems seem to occur in the present and past tenses of *lie:*

Exhausted by writing, he is lying [not laying] down.

After he finished writing, he lay [not laid] down.

Transitive means taking a direct object:

He laid down his pen.

"Now I lie down to sleep" is intransitive, and the verb is *lie.* If you add an object, the verb must be changed: "Now I lay me down to sleep."

Sit and *set* work the same way, but less confusion exists since the forms of the verbs do not overlap: *sit* (usually intransitive; to rest: sit, sat, sat) and *set* (usually transitive; to place: set, set, set).

like/as   Usage of these words, like Caesar's Gaul, is divided, but the conventions of formal writing, as we have seen before, call for *like* before nouns and pronouns, *as* before phrases and clauses.

livid/lurid   Both these words can mean pallid, and both are derived ultimately from colors—*livid* from blue-black, *lurid* from red-yellow. *Lurid* refers to something ghastly or horrible or sensational, or describes an object seen glowing through fire and smoke. *Livid with rage* means pale or ashen, but here physiology seems to be combating etymology. Occasionally people do turn pale with rage, but many get flushed in the face, so *livid* for some users has come to mean red.

mad/angry *Mad* neatly demonstrates the point that we expect writing to be more precise, more careful, more formal than speech. Most educated speakers of English frequently use *mad* to mean "angry"; yet those same speakers, when they become writers, almost unanimously use *mad* only to mean "insane."

one of those who is/one of those who are The handbooks vote for a plural verb in this construction—"She was one of those executives who jog every day"—but usage tends to be divided since the sentence contains both singular and plural indicators ("one" and "executives"). Here the limitations of handbooks and dictionaries can be seen, for they discuss words and phrases in isolation, separate from the contexts that control meaning. It is possible to use either a singular or a plural verb with the *one of those* construction, depending on whether singularity or plurality is emphasized:

Emphasis on one	*Emphasis on many*
He is one of those boys, in fact the only one in his class, who *stays* to help after school.	She is one of those contemporary women who *are* able to manage careers, husbands, children, and households, and still have time for lessons in origami.

only *Only* is a shifty word, which can be placed in many relationships to the concept it modifies. "He only did it for money" is common colloquial English, and can be defended since *only*, early in the sentence, alerts the reader to what follows. Many skilled writers, however, prefer "He did it only for money" on the grounds that *only* modifies "for money," not "did." A game of musical adverbs helps train the ear for these nuances of meaning:

Only he did it for money.

He only did it for money.

He did only it for money.

He did it only for money.

He did it for only money.

He did it for money only.

Absolute rules in these matters of adverbial placement are difficult to formulate. The writer must be alert, often in revision, to the location that best expresses his meaning. A first draft might well read: "The motorcycle was merely taken because it was in the truck when the truck was stolen." The revised version should relocate the *merely:* "The motorcycle was taken merely because it was in the truck when the truck was stolen."

proved/proven *Proved* is commonly used as a past participle (Einstein has proved Planck's quantum theory), *proven* as an adjective (a proven theory).

raise/rear Children formerly were reared; now anything goes.

respectively *Respectively* rarely clarifies, or adds anything other than dead weight. Not even sports writers, who commit almost every other writing sin, would say that "The double-play ball was thrown from Tinker to Evers to Chance, respectively." But a case can be made in certain instances. "After the game, Tinker, Evers, and Chance drank bourbon, beer, and gin respectively." Omitting the *respectively* serves all three drinks to all three players. The difficulty with *respectively*, even in this proper use, is that it works retrospectively. The reader juggles the early elements in a sentence, waiting for guidance. He must reread the sentence to understand it, as the etymology of *respectively* indicates— "look back."

Former and *latter* often cause similar inconvenience. So does the hanging preposition: "The assumptions about and the definition of good writing"; "of, by, and for the people." Reading research has proved that the eyes do not march smoothly along a line of text. They frequently jump back or skip ahead in an effort to find the meaning embedded in strings of words. The writer can facilitate the reader's work by making his text as consecutive as possible, thus reducing the number of backward glances.

split infinitive   The so-called rule against splitting an infinitive concerns the placement of adverbs, as in the case of "only," discussed above. To wildly split an infinitive is an offense, but one against meaning rather than rule. Put the adverb where it makes most sense—inside the infinitive to strongly emphasize the verb, before or after the infinitive to focus significantly on the adverb.

See **Coherence.**

that/which   Some grammarians hold that *that* is restrictive and *which* is nonrestrictive when they are used as relative pronouns:

The amendment that was adopted in 1919 was repealed.

The Prohibition Amendment, which was adopted in 1919, was repealed.

In the first sentence the specific amendment under discussion is defined by the *that* clause; in the second the *which* clause merely inserts additional information. The comma pair supports the distinction between *that* and *which*, between restrictive and nonrestrictive, between a clause that cannot be omitted without changing the meaning of the sentence and one that can.

This neat distinction breaks down somewhat in practice. *That* is necessarily restrictive, but some writers use *which* in both nonrestrictive and restrictive clauses, depending on the fit and feel of the sentence and whether there is another *that* lurking about ("it is that which we fear").

See **Punctuation.**

this   The word *this* is too often cut loose from its referential moorings, especially at the beginning of sentences. This is an unfortunate habit. The word neatly demonstrates the difference between oral and written statements. *This* in speech is often clarified by the presence of the object referred to, and by the speaker's use of a pointing finger, or eyebrow, or hip. In the less tangible, less personal environment of writing, these indicators need to be built out of words. See **Connection** for the use of *this*, when properly followed by a noun, as a transition device.

It demonstrates similar problems and, like *this,* often refers vaguely to something, or everything, that has gone before. "Trite as it may seem, witnessing the tragedy of congenital hearing loss firsthand makes it far clearer." To what does the last *it* refer—the first *it*, witnessing, tragedy, congenital hearing loss? The substance of the sentence dissolves in a mush of possibilities.

unique, more and most   Since the eighteenth century certain words such as *unique* and *perfect* have been thought to be incapable of being modified by adverbs that limit degree. *Rather unique* and *most perfect* are considered substandard in serious prose. According to Fowler, "uniqueness is a matter of yes or no only, no unique thing is more or less unique than another unique thing." Somehow, though, the authors of the Constitution managed to form "a more perfect union."

who/whom Much of the trouble with *who* and *whom* can be eliminated by remembering that the case is governed by the function of the pronoun in its clause, not the function of the clause in the sentence. Identifying the subject of each clause usually solves the problem:

(*I* gave it to the man) (*who* is here.)

(*It* depends on) (*who* is elected.)

(*He* [*who* has clean hands and a pure heart] is saved.)

(*He* [whom *we* washed] is clean.)

Watch out for the red herring dragged across the grammatical trail by phrases such as *she said* or *they thought*, which change nothing:

(*I* gave it to the man) (*who* [*she* said] was here.)

Some of the tangle in using *who* and *whom* stems from overcorrection: "Whom did you say called?" is a more common error than "For who is the book?" Alexander Pope's Pierian principle seems to be at work: A little grammar is a dangerous thing.

Who and *whom* illustrate another general principle of usage. Many problems are not caused by ignorance, but by competing linguistic forces. The average literate American would write "For *whom* is the book?" and would argue that *whom*, as the object of the preposition *for*, must be in the objective case. But that same American will often write, and almost always say, "*Who* is the book for?" Grammatically the two sentences are identical, but in the second the rule calling for the objective case when a pronoun is governed by a preposition tends to be overcome by the strong pull toward the subjective case at the beginning of English sentences.

will/shall   The old rule—"I shall," "you will," "he will" for normal future tense; "I will," "you shall," "he shall" for emphasis—no longer corresponds to general use. Perhaps because *will* is the more common form, *shall* seems now to be the emphatic construction for all personal pronouns, as Douglas MacArthur sensed when he left Corregidor in 1942: "I shall return."

Variety, as Shakespeare's Cleopatra knew, is the way to win an Antony, or a reader:

> If you find him sad,
> Say I am dancing; if in mirth, report
> That I am sudden sick.

Variety provides, in William Cowper's words, the "very spice of life, that gives it all its flavour"—an observation that seems to be as true for writing as for other forms of human activity. Repeating the form of a good sentence has the same danger as repeating a superior meal. Both are pleasing at the first serving, fair when warmed over once, and tiresome if served too many times in succession. A writer needs to have many kinds of good sentences at his command: long and short, general and specific, deductive and inductive, comparative and contrastive, literal and metaphorical, simple and complex, coordinated and subordinated, balanced and eccentric, periodic and cumulative. (A periodic sentence states the main point climactically at the end; the cumulative sentence, more common in ordinary prose, begins with the main point, often stated in a general form, and then proceeds by addition to specify, exemplify, modify, and develop.)

Diversity in rhythm is also important. Take, as an example, the inscription on the monument to the Confederate dead in the town square of Oxford, Mississippi: "They gave their lives in a just and holy cause." Regardless of how one feels about the sentiment, the rhythm of the sentence seems just right. Its balanced finality is based on slight variations. The first part contains two stresses (Thĕy gáve thĕir lívĕs); the second contains three (ĭn ă júst ănd hóly̆ cáuse). In the second part, the two-syllable word "holy" provides relief from the monosyllables that flank it—"just," "and," "cause." The effect would be lost if the two halves marched to the same beat (Thĕy gáve thĕir lívĕs ĭn ă hóly̆ cáuse), or if all the words were flat-footed monosyllables (Thĕy gáve thĕir lívĕs ĭn ă júst ănd góod cáuse), or if a rhythm were established and then overdone (Thĕy gáve thĕir lívĕs ĭn ă cáuse thăt wăs hóly̆ ănd júst).

The principle of variety applies at all levels of composition. Even though repetition is crucial to well-connected writing and is at the heart of most literary devices, readers usually object to words and phrases that are woodenly repeated at close intervals. Words and phrases that are woodenly repeated at close intervals can sometimes be avoided by using slight variants. (This last sentence might better begin "Repeating words and phrases.") Watch out also for accidental rhymes dropped into prose ("Keats makes a striking phrase in praise of beauty.") and for excessive alliteration ("The *Tennessee Code* makes clauses in leases limiting liability invalid."). In two's, alliteration can strongly support the meaning of a sentence; in three's or more it tends to call aggressive and affected attention to itself.

The search for diversity, however, can lead to tangled paths. Substituting words haphazardly to avoid repetition may distort or destroy your meaning. No writer who values his prose or his life would choose at random among *woman, lady, female, wench, wife, mistress, drab, girl, virago, coed*. There are few, if any, exact synonyms in English. Thus if you are looking for alternative wording, use a standard dictionary or Webster's *Dictionary of Synonyms,* which define related words and differentiate among them, rather than a thesaurus, which simply lumps together words generally similar in meaning.

Variety should not be confused with anarchy. Too much variety erodes the cohesiveness of good prose and tumbles the reader into chaos. Too little variety produces boredom, which is just as bad, as the cliché "bored to death" suggests. The writer who wishes to command both his reader's comprehension and his attention must achieve the balance required by all art and be simultaneously faithful to both unity and variety.

Verbs.   "Avoid the passive voice" the writing instructor cries actively, referring to the construction in which the subject receives the action ("the planes were grounded by bad weather") rather than effecting it ("bad weather grounded the planes"). "Avoid" stretches the point to some extent; it depends on whether you are primarily interested in planes or in the weather. But since a passive construction takes longer to read than an active one, and since it often opens the door to vague and general, responsibility-dodging statements ("it was alleged that..."), reserve the passive voice for those few occasions when it is needed.

Be careful also to avoid long strings of sentences slackly woven together by forms of the verb *to be.* Surely Americans—whose ancestors invented such vigorous and colorful verbs as *steamroll, solo, debunk, thumb, bootleg,* and *goose*— can do better than *there is, there are, it is, it was.* Often a sentence can be strengthened and shortened at the same time:

The Personnel Commission, in its ruling that Ms. Best could be demoted without right of appeal, was in excess of its authority and was in violation of due process of law.	The Personnel Commission, in its ruling that Ms. Best could be demoted without right of appeal, exceeded its authority and violated due process of law.

Psycholinguist James Deese suggests that the verb exerts the greatest energy in a sentence since it gives the most information. The noun subject simply names the actor or the setting; the verb tells what happens, what is new. Strengthening the verb in a sentence thus may well be the shortest path to improving the sentence as a whole.

See **Adjectives and adverbs, Conciseness.**

Weak intensifiers are props for sagging prose: *absolutely, actually, awfully, basically, definitely, extremely, fairly, indeed, in fact, interesting, literally, overwhelming, perfectly, quite, rather, really, so, very.* Often such words boomerang and intensify the weaknesses they were meant to correct. "An enjoyable experience" and "in my opinion" are bad enough by themselves. "A very enjoyable experience" and "definitely in my opinion" are worse. *Literally* often means nothing ("she was literally exhausted") and occasionally turns inside out to mean figuratively ("she was literally dead on her feet").

Unearned emphasis creeps into structure as well as word choice. Journalists and advertisers exaggerate significance and quality by stating a superlative and then tacking on a qualifier: "Few people realize just how pervasive an ingredient salt has become in the modern American diet.... It is the nation's leading food additive after sugar." Accidents and tragedies are regularly pumped up by formula to make the day's news more engrossing: It is the nation's worst (air disaster, coal strike, mass murder) since (1978, World War II, last week).

Writers who depend on italics (underlining in typing) to intensify their meaning are *usually*, but not *always*, compensating for weak prose. Emphasis has to be earned and cannot merely be decreed.

Afterword

Good writing demands a willing spirit, for no writer or pianist or shortstop learns his trade simply by doing mechanical exercises. You must be interested in your subject and in trying to express it. If your project bores you, it will lobotomize your reader.

If you have difficulty beginning, consider why you are writing, what you have to say, how you wish to present yourself, and whom you are addressing. Selecting and grouping the points you wish to make and considering different strategies of presentation can relieve compositional constipation. A rough outline may help. But don't spend all your energy in advance. Get writing while your ideas are still being formed, before your research is completed. Research is seldom finished; the procrastinator can always find another book to read or case to review. And the act of writing will itself help focus your ideas and direct the search for additional material. Technique, as Mark Shorer puts it, is discovery.

Many writers are hesitant to begin because their first sentences fail to achieve the high standards they set for their projects. First drafts seldom do. Pitch in anyway, and don't be finical about small details of correctness or polish. Much expert writing begins with a swiftly written, ungrammatical, ellipsis-filled rough draft that captures the flow of ideas and sketches out the main sections and their relationships. Correctness, completeness, precise wording—all these can be attended to during revision, just as a carpenter fills in braces and shims after the framing is complete.

Good carpenters are made as well as born, and they are made through constant practice. Writing is a complex skill, learned through doing. In many ways it has more in common with repairing a motorcycle or skiing than with learning a body of knowledge, such as history. You cannot learn to conquer slalom gates or paragraph connections by reading a book. You must strap on your skis, or your pencil, and push off across the deceptive, exhilarating, confidence-testing surface of white.

But practice is not enough; performance must be criticized to be improved. An instructor is an obvious critic, especially one interested in analyzing your writing, not just in grading or correcting or labeling it. (An army of English teachers filling millions of margins with *awk, frag, ref, agr, pn, gr,* and *dm* have kept themselves harmlessly occupied in America, but without, I suspect, substantially affecting the quality of their students' writing.) There are other choices. A classmate, friend, or business colleague, even if he or she is not an expert writer, can usually point out incomprehensible and infelicitous passages. And the writer himself, if he will let his paper cool off, will find that he returns to his work with a more rigorous eye, with less tolerance for defects than during his original inspiration. The enthusiasms of midnight, whether devoted to writing or romancing, often look different in the sober light of the next day. And reading aloud, to yourself if no one else will listen, helps provide the distance necessary for effective criticism.

Index

Listed are main entries (boldface), words and expressions discussed specifically (italics), and names and topics.

Abbreviations, 29–31
Absolute expressions, 1
Abstract language. See **Specific details.**
Acronyms, 81
Active verbs. See **Verbs.**
Addams, Jane, quoted, 65
Adjectives and adverbs, 1
Adverb placement, 7–8, 88
Adverbs. See **Adjectives and adverbs; Weak intensifiers.**
Aggravate/irritate, 83
Agreement, 8, 60–61
A historian/an historian, 83
Aitchison, Jean, 38
Alliteration, 93
Ambiguity, 1–3, 46
Analogy. See **Metaphor.**
Antecedent, 59–60
Anti, 45
Apostrophe, 64–65
Argumentation, 79
Assassin, etymology of, 20
Atrocious, etymology of, 23
Attributive noun (noun-noun construction), 43
Auspicious, etymology of, 19
Awful, etymology of, 23

Baugh, Albert C., 38
Belittle, etymology of, 20
Between/among, 83
Bibliographic forms. See **Footnote and bibliographic forms.**
Brackets, 69
Brandt, Robert, 41
By and large, etymology of, 19

Cable, Thomas, 38
Capitalization, 3–4, 70

Churchill, Winston, 56–57, 75
Citation. See **Footnote and bibliographic forms.**
Clemens, Samuel L., 24, 48–50, 58–59, 73–74
Clichés, 4–7
Coherence, 7–10. See also **Ambiguity; Paragraphing; Thesis.**
Coinage of new words. See **Neologism.**
Collective nouns and pronouns, 60–61
Colloquial language. See **Clichés; Jargon; Slang.**
Colon, 63, 65
Comma
comma pair, 63–64, 89–90
comma splice, 62–63
with quotation marks, 69, 81
in series, 65–66
Commager, Henry Steele, 53–56
Compare to/compare with, 83
Compound adjectives, 66
Conciseness, 10–13. See also **Adjectives and adverbs; Jargon; Latinisms.**
Conclusions, 31, 52
Concreteness. See **Specific details.**
Conjunctions, 13–14
Connection, 13–16
Connotation, 59
Consistency, 8, 9–10
Conspiracy, etymology of, 19
Contrast, 55–56
Correctness. See **Proofreading.**
Cowper, William, 92
Crews, Frederick, 37

Dangling modifier, 8, 87–88
Dangling preposition, 88–89

Dash, 63–64, 66, 81
Data is/data are, 83
Debauch, etymology of, 20
Deduction, 75
Deese, James, 95
Deprecate/depreciate, 84
Description, 79
Dickinson, Emily, 25
Diction. See **Clichés; Jargon;
     Latinisms; Neologism;
     Precision; Punctuation**
     (quotation marks); **Slang;
     Specific details**.
Dictionaries, 17–19, 93–94. See also
     Precision.
Dictionaries of usage, 38
Dilapidate, etymology of, 20
Disaster, etymology of, 19
Disraeli, Benjamin, 66
Documentation. See **Quotations;
     Footnote and bibliographic
     forms**.
Double expressions, 12
Double negative, 35–36
Due to, 84

Egregious, etymology of, 21
Either/or and *and/or*, 84
Ellipsis, 68–69
Emerson, Ralph W., quoted, 8
Emphasis, 70, 95–96
Ending with a preposition, 84
Enthusiasm, etymology of, 19
Etc., 84
Etymology, 19–24
Evans, Bergen, 38
Evans, Cornelia, 38
Exceptions, 24–25
Exclamation point, 66
Exposition, 79. See also
     **Literary writing and
     expository writing**.
Expository writing. See **Literary
     writing and expository writing**.

False comparative, 26
Farther/further, 84
Fewer/less, 85

Figurative language. See **Metaphor**.
First draft. See **Revision**.
Focus. See **Coherence; Thesis**.
Follett, Wilson, 38
Footnote and bibliographic forms,
     26–31
Foreign terms, use of italics with, 81
Form and content, 31–32
Former/latter, 89
Fowler, Henry W., 38
Fragment, 63
French, in the history of English, 44
Fused sentence (comma splice), 62–63
Fussell, Paul, 68

Gender. See **Sexist language**.
Generalization. See **Specific details**.
Grammar. See **Grammar, usage, and
     style**.
Grammar, usage, and style, 32–37
Gung ho, etymology of, 19

Handbooks, 37–39
Hanged/hung, 85
Harass, 82
Heller, Joseph, 52
Helpmate, etymology of, 20
Hermaphrodite, etymology of, 20
Hibachi, etymology of, 19
Hirsch, E.D., Jr., 39, 76
History of English, 33–36, 38
Holiday, etymology of, 19
Homonyms, 39–40
Hopefully, 85
Hopkins, Gerard Manley, 50
Humor, etymology of, 24
Hyphen, 66, 81

*I am not so careful as/I am not as
     careful as*, 85
I feel bad/I feel badly, 85
If I were he/if I was he, 85
Imply/infer, 85
Indefinite article, 83
Indentation, 68, 81
Induction, 75
Inflection, 33–34
Initials, 81

Interpretative/interpretive, 85
Interrelatedness. See **Coherence**.
Intransitive verb, 86
Introductions, 31, 51–52
It, 90
Italic type, 81, 96
It is I/It is me, 86
Its/it's, 64
-ize, as suffix, 50–51

James, Henry, 32, 49–50, 69–70
Jargon, 40–43
Jeep, etymology of, 20
Jonson, Ben, 70

Kain, Richard, 62
Kelly, Walt, quoted, 74
King, Martin Luther, Jr., 57
Knave, etymology of, 21

Lamberts, J.J., 35–36
Latinisms, 43–45
Lewd, etymology of, 21
Lie/lay, 86
Like/as, 86
Literary writing and expository writing, 45–47. See also **Exceptions**.
Livid/lurid, 86–87
Logic. See **Coherence**.
Lowell, Amy, 62
Lynch, etymology of, 21

MacArthur, Douglas, 92
McPhee, John, 69
Mad/angry, 87
Margins, 81
Maroon, etymology of, 22
Martin, Leonard, quoted, 15–16
Mencken, H.L., 38, 72
Metaphor, 47–50
Milic, Louis T., 24–25
Misplaced modifier, 8, 87–88
Mistakes. See **Proofreading**.
Modifiers, 1, 8, 87–88
Ms., 71–72

Narration, 79
Neologism, 50–51

Nicholson, Margaret, 38
Nocent, etymology of, 22
Nonrestrictive clause, 63–64, 89–90
Noun adjuncts (nouns modifying other nouns), 43
Numbers, 51

Obvious statements, 51–52. See also **Conciseness**.
O.K., etymology of, 22
Old English, 33–35, 43–44
One of those who is/one of those who are, 87
Only, 87–88
Order. See **Coherence**.
Organization. See **Coherence; Thesis**.
Overcorrection, 91
Overstatement, 74
Oxford English Dictionary, 17

Panic, etymology of, 19
Paragraphing, 52–56. See also **Coherence; Typing conventions**.
Parallelism, 56–58. See also **Connection**.
Parenthesis, 64, 67
Passive voice, 94
Pejoration, 21
Poe, Edgar Allan, 78
Poetry, in quotations, 68
Point of view, 8
Pooley, Robert C., 38
Possessive, 64–65
Potter, David M., 48
Precision, 58–59. See also **Proofreading**.
Preposition, ending with, 84
Pretty, etymology of, 21
Prevent, etymology of, 23
Pronouns, 59–61, 64. See also **Sexist language**.
Proofreading, 61–62
Proved/proven, 88
Puffery, 62
Punctuation, 62–67

Quotation marks, 67, 68–69, 80, 81
Quotations, 68–70

Raise/rear, 88
Redundancy. See **Conciseness**.
Repetition, 13, 14, 57–58, 92–93
Respectively, 88–89
Restrictive clause, 63–64, 89–90
Revision, 70–71, 97–98
Rhythm, 93
Russell, Bertrand, 65

Sanguine, etymology of, 24
Semicolon, 67
Sentence fragment, 63
Sentence structure, 92
Series
 for rhetorical effect, 58
 use of comma in, 65–66
Sexist language, 60, 71–72
Shakespeare, William, 24, 31, 56–57, 70, 92
Shaughnessy, Mina P., 39
Shaw, George Bernard, 57–58, 77
Shorer, Mark, 97
Shrewd, etymology of, 21
Sideburns, etymology of, 19
Silly, etymology of, 21
Sit/set, 86
Slang, 72–74
Smith, Frank, 61–62
Specific details, 74–76
Speech and writing, 76
Spelling, 61, 76–78
Split infinitive, 89
Standard English, 36
Stark naked, etymology of, 22
Stevenson, Adlai, 74
Strunk, William, Jr., 38
Style, 36–37
Subjunctive, 85
Supercilious, etymology of, 19
Syntax, 33–34

Taxi, etymology of, 22
Teddy bear, etymology of, 19

That/which, 89–90
Thesis, 78–80
This, 90
Thoreau, Henry David, 36–37
Titles, 31, 80
Tomahawk, etymology of, 19
Tone, 8
Topic. See **Thesis**.
Transition. See **Connection**.
Transitive verb, 86
Trivia, etymology of, 23
Trudgill, Peter, 36
Twain, Mark. See Clemens.
Type, 50
Typing conventions, 80–81

Understatement, 74
Unique, more and most, 90–91
Unity. See **Coherence**.
Usage. See **Grammar, usage, and style**; **Usage: some particular cases**.
Usage: some particular cases, 81–92

Vague expressions. See **Clichés**; **Specific details**.
Variety, 92–94
Verbs, 94–95
Versus, 45
Via, 45

Weak intensifiers, 95–96
Weathers, Winston, 58
Webster, Daniel, 68–69
Whiskey, etymology of, 23
White, E.B., 38
Who/whom, 91–92
Will/shall, 92
-wise, as suffix, 50–51
Word division, 81
Wordiness. See **Conciseness**; **Precision**; **Puffery**.
Word order, 33–34

C D E F G H I J
0 1 2 3 4 5 6 7 8 9